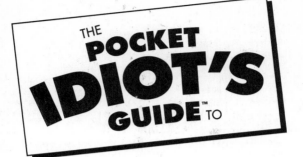

THE POCKET IDIOT'S GUIDE TO

Being a Groom

Third Edition

by Jennifer Lata Rung and Mark Rung

ALPHA

A member of Penguin Group (USA) Inc.

Contents

Appendixes

Introduction

So You're Ready to Take the Plunge

We know you're no idiot. In fact, if you're reading this book, you must be pretty smart. That's because you're wise enough to know exactly what you *don't* know—and that's weddings. It's okay that you don't know; you're not supposed to. Unlike your fiancée, you were not born and bred with the divine knowledge of all things nuptial—nor do you want to pore through book after thick bridal book looking for the information you need. Whether you're searching for ideas on gifts for your groomsmen, how to budget for a wedding, or what you need to do to get a marriage license, we've compiled all the necessary information to be your one-stop resource.

Thirty years ago, you wouldn't have needed this book. Chances are your father had little or nothing to do with planning a wedding and frankly can't believe that you would, either. But as you know, times have changed—and whether your fiancée is a strict traditionalist or assumes that the planning will be strictly 50/50, there's information in this book to help you. What better way to impress your bride than to tell her where the wedding ring originated? Or help her choose a photographer? Or even better, use one of our wedding-gift suggestions for your bride?

How to Use This Book

The book is designed to offer all the information you need with the minimum effort necessary to get it. If you need advice on a certain topic, simply refer to the table of contents. If you need a serious but quick briefing on the bigger picture, take a breeze through each chapter. Within, you'll find the following features offering little snacks of information for the times you're not hungry for the whole enchilada.

Groom Gambit

This is quick, bite-sized information that will provide you with money-saving, efficiency-gaining, and fool-proofing tips to sufficiently impress your bride, your family, and your future in-laws.

Nuptial No-Nos

You're engaged now, so you're probably accustomed to hearing the word "no"—or at least being told what to do. Well, this feature will tell you what not to do to avoid losing your shirt, losing respect—or losing your mind.

Wedding Words _____

> You haven't had this much trouble under-
> standing another human being since
> eighth-grade Spanish. Fear no more:
> Wedding Words are here to help you
> get to the bottom of confusing wedding
> jargon.

Acknowledgments

To my own groom, already more than five years
beyond your title role … and to our expanding
family. Time does fly when we're having fun ….

Trademarks

All terms mentioned in this book that are known to
be or are suspected of being trademarks or service
marks have been appropriately capitalized. Alpha
Books and Penguin Group (USA) Inc. cannot attest
to the accuracy of this information. Use of a term
in this book should not be regarded as affecting the
validity of any trademark or service mark.

Chapter 1

So She's the One: Welcome to Couplehood

In This Chapter

- Why do you need a book?
- The definition of "groom"
- Exactly what components go into planning a wedding?
- Have you made the right decision?

Well, the hard work is over. You studied and scrutinized to find just the right engagement ring; you sweated and stuttered when talking to her father about your intentions; you even got down on bended knee and (although there's no need to admit this) shed a tear when she said yes. The rest is smooth sailing. All you have left to say is "I do" and head out for that honeymoon, right? Wrong!

You've got a long road ahead of you, and you've barely left the exit ramp. Being a groom means a lot more than just showing up these days. But hold on: I'm here to make this whole event as smooth as possible. So grab a beer, sit back, and prepare for the ride.

Why a Groom's Guide?

In just a generation or two, weddings and the preparation leading up to them have changed drastically. It's rare these days to experience what was normal in our parents' day—the blushing bride, barely out of her teens, swept away by her handsome groom from her parents' home.

How Many Cattle Is Your Bride Bringing to the Marriage?

In the days when gender roles were more finely drawn, traditions developed. The bride's parents paid the lion's share of the wedding expenses, theoretically as a sort of *dowry* before her husband began supporting her financially.

Wedding Words

A **dowry** is historically an offering of cash, gifts, or a combination of both from the bride's family to the groom, to make the transaction more "worthwhile."

Of course, with the money also came most of the input and veto power. Traditions such as pre-wedding showers were in place to help the young couple set up their home with dishes, linens, and appliances. Nowadays, many couples already have two households full of most of the things they need. A pre-wedding pow-wow of the couple's parents used to be a way to introduce them to one another, as well as provide a forum to make any additional wedding-related financial arrangements. Today, this is more complicated, with more couples living far away from the places where they grew up, and with divorces and stepfamilies complicating the issue even further.

Closing (or Retaining) Gender Gaps

With all the social changes of the past 30 or 40 years have come inevitable changes in wedding tradition—and particularly in the groom's wedding role. Formerly, most grooms left the planning to the brides and their families and showed up to events as they were told. But now, many grooms have more of a financial stake in their own weddings—and working women and their working mothers don't have the free time they once did to pore over guest lists and invitations for days on end. The tricky part comes with knowing when to adhere to tradition—and when to break it. This book is meant to help grooms work with their brides for an arrangement that will best suit their particular situations.

The best advice we'll give is to adopt a strategy that works for you. In all likelihood, this is the largest "project" that the two of you have worked on to date—and learning how to work together and compromise now is a great starting point for a lifetime of relative harmony. With a little diplomacy and sensitivity, you'll figure out a system that works best for you as a couple. Your bride might want to plan every last detail and just let you show up; if that's okay with you, then go for it. However, your bride might really need your help, too, in which case you should be prepared to lend a hand.

Groom Gambit _____

> You should view your wedding planning much the same way you would view a project at work. When you begin partnering on a project with someone, you are generally a bit sensitive right away to the other person's working habits and style.

What Is a Groom?

A groom is just a guy on his wedding day, right? Wrong. Traditional definitions of the word *groom* define him as an engaged man up to and including his wedding day and for some time afterward. This means that a groom's duties don't begin and end on his wedding day; rather, his commitment and responsibilities kick in from the moment he's engaged.

We know that until now you've probably experienced an extended adolescence that has entailed drinking with the boys until all hours, sleeping until noon when you feel like it, and "postponing" laundry and dishwashing until it's convenient or until mold grows on the dishes, whichever comes first—in general, the minimum effort necessary to maintain your three basic needs of food, shelter, and beer.

Wedding Words

The Webster's II New Riverside Pocket Dictionary has some other definitions for **groom**—"to make neat and trim, brush," and "to train." Funny how a word once reserved for horse hygiene has evolved to personify a man getting married.

The Transition from Foal to Stallion

Here's where the "to train" part of the definition of "groom" enters the picture. Certainly, you will not become Mr. Cleaver overnight; some residual bachelor revelry will almost certainly remain in your system for a good long time. However, it is customary to add some semblance of responsibility to your life—a full-time job, perhaps, or all-night partying cut back to just one night a week—you know, the basics. If you want to be the "perfect" groom, now's the time to really shine for your bride and your in-laws-to-be. Work a little harder for that promotion so that her dad will rest easy, knowing she'll never want for that yearly trip to the tropics—or a roof over her head. Put her before your buddies every once in a while so that she continues to believe she made the right decision. Stash a little money away each month to save for the house or the furniture you desperately need to replace. In other words, become the man you've always had buried somewhere deep within you.

Nuptial No-Nos

> Don't assume that just because she's got the ring, your job is finished. Your bride will welcome—and appreciate—any assistance you can give her during wedding planning, even if it's just happily agreeing to look at some reception sites with her. In other words, the courtship ain't over yet.

Of course, this preparation is the mental game involved in being a groom. There are all sorts of practical, day-to-day tasks you must complete, help out with, or at least consult upon. That activity is what this book will help you get straight.

Your Engagement—What's in Store

Women generally know a lot about what's involved in weddings well before they're engaged. They're socialized to know—and be excited about—all things nuptial. Chances are, your bride has already been closely involved in a friend's or sister's wedding, so she has a basic knowledge of what's necessary. But you—well, we know you've probably done all you can to avoid the trappings of weddings until now. Not only are weddings girl stuff, but they are also very, very frightening. But now that you're planning your own wedding, we're sure you'll want all the necessary information to have the best party—and find the greatest deals—possible.

Check out this quick list of the elements involved in planning a wedding:

- Setting a date
- Setting a budget
- Introducing your parents to each other
- Choosing your best man
- Choosing your groomsmen
- Attending an engagement party
- Creating a guest list
- Creating a wedding-day seating plan (for sit-down style weddings)
- Registering for gifts
- Choosing a ceremony site
- Choosing a reception site
- Choosing the music
- Choosing the decorations and flowers
- Choosing your tux style

- Finding adequate wedding-day transportation (limousine, antique Rolls, or whatever)
- Finding and hiring a photographer
- Finding and hiring a videographer
- Choosing your reception menu items
- Choosing and purchasing a wedding band for your bride
- Choosing a wedding gift for your bride
- Planning the rehearsal dinner
- Acquiring a marriage license
- Getting a blood test
- Choosing a honeymoon destination and planning your honeymoon
- Finding a place to live
- Furnishing the place where you'll live

So you wondered why you need a book on this stuff? Don't fret; we'll break it all down for you, step by step, so that by the time your wedding rolls around, *you'll* be the expert.

Did You Make the Right Decision?

Yeah, yeah, it just feels right, right? Plus she's been badgering you relentlessly for a ring for what seems at least as long as sitting through a chick flick—*with* subtitles. But before you go any further, a little self-reflection might be fun. Take our quiz to see whether you're making the right decision:

1. The two of you have plans to go out Friday night with a group of friends; you get the flu. Does she …

    A. Go out anyway and come in at 3 A.M., waking you up to tell you how much fun she had?

    B. Get mad at you for ruining your plans, and tell you you'd better start taking care of yourself?

    C. Come over to your place, make chicken soup, and put wet compresses on your head?

2. You forget to mention until Sunday morning that your mother has invited the two of you over for Sunday dinner. You know she doesn't have plans. Does she …

    A. Refuse to go on principle?

    B. Go with you but pout and complain all night to the wonderment of your parents?

    C. Graciously accept the invitation?

3. It's Friday and the two of you have plans for dinner. Your best friend calls to tell you his girlfriend has left him for another guy. He really needs a shoulder right now. Does she …

    A. Tell your friend you'll give him a call—*after* you get home from dinner and a movie?

    B. Reschedule your plans until Saturday so you and your friend can talk?

C.   Make him dinner and set up your guest room for him for a few days so he won't be lonely?

4. Does she …

A.   Call her father "Daddy" and refer often to his money?

B.   Call her father a "jerk" and obsess over him in tri-weekly sessions with her therapist?

C.   Call her father "Dad" and occasionally ask his advice or tell him she loves him?

5. Does a "night out with the girls" mean …

A.   She shops for a week to find just the right skimpy black cocktail dress and strappy heels?

B.   You'll have to hear the next day how she ran into Christopher, her old "friend" from college—"and he was wearing a Rolex, and he just sold his business to Microsoft, and he *loves* sushi?"

C.   Popcorn and *Desperate Housewives* at her best friend's?

The scoring is simple. If you answered one or more As or Bs, you might be in trouble, pal—or your fiancée's selfish behavior is the result of a communication breakdown between the two of you. All hope is not lost; read Chapter 7 for communication strategies useful for engagement and well beyond.

Walking in Her Shoes

According to most brides, the perfect groom is not a man who already knows everything he has to do. He's someone who understands the amount of work that goes into planning a wedding and who will be patient and communicative throughout the process. The perfect groom is also there to whisk her off for margaritas and dancing when things get too crazy after a long week of extra hours at the office, an argument with a friend, and the DJ's revelation that he double-booked and can't provide the music for the wedding.

 Groom Gambit

As an engaged man, you will slowly but surely witness the evolution of the pronoun "I" into "we" as you move closer to your wedding date. Seemingly this natural phenomenon has its roots in Darwinian theory—only the fittest survive.

Keep in mind that patience is the key word during planning a wedding. She's going to be talking a lot about things like colors, flowers, and her mother's dress—things as foreign to you as the Lifetime Channel. Just hear her out and make suggestions about the stuff you do care about—the music, the limo, and budgetary decisions. She'll appreciate the input and the listening ear.

Chapter 2

Pre-Game Strategy: Budgets You Can Work With

In This Chapter

- Determining who pays for what
- What will our families contribute?
- A breakdown of specific wedding expenses
- Choosing what type of wedding you'll have
- Setting the wedding date

The games are about to begin. But first, you must develop a strategic plan (think Xs and Os on a blackboard, if that's easier) to be sure you're in the best possible shape for game day. Your bride and her family are the Xs; you and yours are the Os. It's tough to say exactly where the Xs are gonna end up at the end of each play, but you can create some possible scenarios to develop your counter-attack. That's what you'll find in this chapter—"O" scenarios that are most comfortable for you, your bride, and your families.

But isn't this wedding stuff all about being on the same team? Eventually, yes. First, you've got to create the best possible situation for both parties—and then you're free to unite. Shift your thinking for a moment to consider two corporate entities merging. Before two companies come together, they're going to make sure that both their interests are represented—especially those of a financial nature. Only then will the X company and O company become XO, Inc.

Okay, enough with the sports/business/love metaphors and on to some concrete info.

Budgeting!

It's probably the first time you've seen budgeting and an exclamation point on the same page, right? We thought it might be nice to imbue some enthusiasm into a task that's about as palatable as a rice cake for dinner. Actually, budgeting doesn't have to be all bad (especially if the bride's parents have offered to foot the entire bill), but only if you treat it as you would any other financial arrangement—with practicality and good planning.

 Groom Gambit _____

> Before you and your bride even start putting figures in your budget, you need to decide just what type of wedding you're going to have and how much (if any) each set of parents is going to contribute.

After the heady glow of the first few days of engagement, your parents will probably bring up the subject of wedding finances. Traditional etiquette deems that the bride's parents pay for most of the wedding expenses, and the groom's pay for some additional items. Here's the traditional breakdown:

Bride and family:

- Engagement party (if one is held by bride's family)
- Groom's ring
- Wedding gift for the groom
- Paper items, including invitations, stationery, thank-you cards, and wedding programs (the printed booklets you give guests at the ceremony)
- Bridal gown and Mother's and Father's wedding-day attire
- Flowers for church or temple and reception
- Bouquets for bridesmaids and flower girls
- Church or synagogue fees, ceremony music, and other ceremony expenses
- Wedding and engagement photography and videography
- Transportation of bridal party to ceremony and reception
- All reception costs, including food, drink, room or hall rental fees, decorations, and music

Groom and family:

- Engagement party (if one is held by groom's family)
- Bride's engagement and wedding rings
- Wedding gift for the bride
- Rehearsal dinner
- Groom's tuxedo and parents' attire
- Bride's bouquet, boutonnieres for groomsmen, and corsages for mothers and grandmothers
- Marriage license
- Clergy's fee
- Honeymoon

Additional expenses to share or divide:

- Both families can pay for the reception or the rehearsal dinner if the bride or groom's family is unable to bear the entire cost alone.
- The families might offer to purchase the bridesmaids' dresses and accessories and groomsmen's rentals.
- The bride's family may buy all the flowers.
- Both families may split photography and videography.
- Additional costs include transportation and lodging for out-of-town guests.
- The groom's family can offer to cover specific reception costs such as liquor and hors d'oeuvres.

Unless you're flying on the Concorde, staying at the Ritz-Carlton, and taking an extended trip for your honeymoon, it's pretty obvious that the expenses weigh heavily on the bride's family's side if you're following traditional etiquette.

What Does This Traditional Budget Stuff Mean to You?

Here's where wedding planning in the twenty-first century gets tricky. Like the breakdown in traditional planning duties, the breakdown in who pays for what isn't as clear-cut as it once was. A couple who has been out of school and working for a few years will most likely have the resources to pay for some or all of their own wedding expenses, and more and more often are choosing to do so. This enables them to retain control over the planning as well as avoid burdening their parents with yet another expense. Feel free to flout the financial conventions outlined above; they are merely presented as a traditional guideline. Obviously, you should do what makes the most sense for you as a couple, and for your families.

 Groom Gambit _____

The budget is the first serious conversation about your wedding that you'll have with your bride—to determine what each family's contribution will be, if any, and to decide how you'll want to pay for it.

How to Approach Family

Presumably, your families are savvy enough to bring up the subject of *wedding finances* with *you* before you need to bring it up with *them*. Perhaps there's already a "financial understanding" in each of your families, based on older siblings who've had weddings. Maybe your bride's family has always told her that they'll pay for her whole wedding. These are the easiest-case scenarios. But it can become uncomfortable if your parents never broach the topic, and you're left to wonder what, if any, they'll be willing to cover. This leaves you with a couple of options: You can either approach them (with delicacy and diplomacy) to see if they can swing anything, or simply plan on paying for everything yourselves. Then, if they offer later, you'll already be ahead of the game.

Wedding Words

When it comes to **wedding finances,** don't assume that either set of parents will pay for anything wedding-related until they tell you so. Be sensitive to their financial situation, and speak to them as an adult, not as a spoiled child "entitled" to their patronage.

Nitty-Gritty Budgeting

Okay, here's the tough part. Wedding expenses range drastically, depending on the type of wedding you're having, where you're having it, and how many people you're inviting. You might be planning a simple backyard wedding with a punch-and-cookies reception or a traditional, full-blown evening reception for 350 guests at the nicest place in town. It's actually a catch-22: Budget dictates what type of wedding you'll have, and what type of wedding you want will determine budget parameters. It's up to you to decide whether the chicken or the egg comes first.

Your first option is to decide what type of wedding you want, factor in parental contributions, and then determine how much you'll need to save. Based on these calculations you can then set a date to accommodate your savings plan.

Your other option, if you're paying for part or all of your wedding yourselves, is to decide on a budgetary figure before you even think about what type of wedding you want. For example, if together you want to spend $5,000, you can use that figure to decide where you'll have it, what kind of food and drink you'll serve, and how many people you'll invite. If you decide on 40 guests, $5,000 will buy you a pretty elegant affair. If you want 250 guests, think more in the cookout range (or cocktails only).

Nuptial No-Nos

> Don't forget that you and your bride have the ultimate power to decide what's important. Don't buy into every wedding product or service you see.

Here are some of the specific components you need to consider when budgeting for a traditional wedding. Obviously, each wedding is individual, and you can decide to eschew any of these items (or elope, for that matter). Beware of the firehose level of pressure you'll encounter from the wedding industry, hawking their wares at an emotional time.

Costs vary widely for the following. Check with friends and local vendors for ballpark figures in your area, and then set your own parameters:

- Rehearsal dinner
- Ceremony fees, including clergy and musician's fees
- Reception food
- Reception bar
- Reception music (live versus DJ makes a huge financial difference)
- Wedding attire—bridal gown and formal men's attire
- Flowers and other decorative items (more expensive than you'd think)
- Photography and videography

- Transportation (limo from ceremony to reception, "getaway" car)
- Wedding invitations and thank-you stationery
- Wedding-day program
- Wedding bands
- Gifts for wedding attendants
- Gifts for each other
- Overnight accommodations for you and your bride
- Subsidizing wedding party expenses, such as bridesmaids' dresses, groomsmen's tux rentals, and accommodations (certainly not mandatory, unless you're Richard Branson and/or you've demanded that they wear couture)
- Additional expenses (wedding favors, grooming expenses such as haircuts, and so on)
- Honeymoon

Choosing Your Wedding Style

There are as many types of weddings as potential brides to choose from (seemingly endless, but when it comes right down to it, quite limited by your sound, practical judgment and parents' approval). Now that you've established your budget, you'll consider your options; in other words, you're not obligated to spend thousands of dollars on a generic hall punctuated by 200 guests, mediocre food, and your drunk college friends hitting on your (not-so-little-anymore) sister. Nor are you expected to max out your credit card and hock your stereo to pay for flowers that have a one-day life span. If you're lucky enough to have carte blanche, however, there are options here to suit you as well.

Some of your options include the following styles:

- **Outdoor.** An outdoor, casual wedding such as a clambake or cookout on the beach or at a park, with plenty of spirits, good friends, and family.

- **Small but elegant.** A small, elegant affair of 50-ish guests with immediate family and very close friends. Use the money you're saving from limiting the guest list to pay for excellent food and an unforgettable venue.

- **Nontraditional.** A nontraditional site such as an art gallery, historical museum, or landmark location that offers guests a unique experience they'll always remember.

- **Destination wedding.** A destination wedding (becoming more popular), where you and close family and friends spend a week or long weekend in a special location away from home—with the getaway highlighted by your exchanged vows. You may offer to pay for some or part of your guests' costs in lieu of incurring traditional wedding expenses.

- **Weekend wedding.** Ideal for larger budgets and a lot of out-of-town guests. Give your guests a weekend they won't forget by hosting weekend-long events in addition to the traditional rehearsal dinner and wedding. Plan a full slate of activities such as a sightseeing excursion, golf outing, beach party, or outdoor barbecue for your guests so that they'll have something to do before and after the wedding festivities.

- **Cocktail/champagne reception.** A daytime cake-and-champagne-toast-only wedding or an evening cocktails-only reception to save money on food. (Be careful with this one; many guests expect to be served a meal at a wedding, so make it clear on the invitation that there will be no brunch, lunch, or dinner. Also, be prepared for the inevitable naysayers.)

- **At home.** A home-catered event, with relatives and friends doing the cooking to save money.

Clearly, any variation of these styles can be combined with your own creativity for an event that fits both your budget and your personal style—an event that none of your guests will ever forget. Plus you'll avoid all that cookie-cutter, chicken-dance, I-can't-even-sit-with-my-date rigmarole.

Setting the Date

Now that you've got your projected budget and an idea of the type of wedding you want, it will be easier to set a date for the wedding. The following are some variables to consider when setting the date that you'll celebrate for the next 50-plus years (until you rejoin your gender and begin forgetting after the first couple of anniversaries):

- **Season.** Time of year you prefer—winter, spring, fall, or summer. Keep in mind that if you don't have a long engagement, it's tougher to get the place, photographer, and band you want in late spring, summer, and early fall because that's when everyone else is getting married, too.

- **Location.** Where your wedding will take place. If it's out of town, be sure to factor in enough time for long-distance planning and travel back and forth beforehand.

- **Timing.** How long you'd like your engagement to be—most vital in "shotgun" situations. In other, less intense situations, you should determine whether it's important to you to plan and marry right away, or if job or personal considerations make it more practical to have a longer engagement.

- **Conflicts.** Other family events, such as relatives' weddings or milestone occasions like anniversaries, which could potentially conflict with your event. Be considerate. If your grandparents are inviting a lot of out-of-town guests for their fiftieth wedding anniversary in August, don't expect those same people to fly back to town in September.

- **Holidays.** Don't forget to consider a range of religious holidays if you're inviting guests of different faiths. You might get more regrets if you choose to hold your wedding on a holiday or holiday weekend, when people may have other plans or obligations.

Nuptial No-Nos

One groom insisted that he and his bride plan their wedding for December 31, 1999. It was great for close family and friends—but more casual acquaintances wanted to be with *their* close family and friends for the turn of the millennium. You'll get a lot of guests' regrets if you don't consider others' priorities when setting a date.

The Cast

In This Chapter

- Choosing your best man
- Other honorary positions
- Choosing clergy
- Creating a guest list

Whether you're usually a total attention-monger or a behind-the-scenes kinda guy, your wedding day will inevitably mean one thing. It's your bride's starring role, and you're the Nick Lachey to her Jessica Simpson. In other words, expect to be in the spotlight—as well as act as casting director for supporting roles like best man, groomsmen, and all those lucky extras who'll be eating your food and drinking your wine.

Does Your Best Man Really Have to Be Better?

The whole concept of choosing one best man goes against the general grain of guyness. Unlike girls, who grew up with the need to publicly identify their best friend du jour, guys are more content to hang with a group, avoiding titles and labels—although there generally is one person who he's closer to than the others. This can be a brother, a childhood friend, a cousin—even your father. This is who should become your *best man*.

Wedding Words _____

The **best man** is the person closest to the groom, chosen to carry out helpful wedding-related duties and to provide support.

Choosing Your Best Man

The best man is probably the most high-profile member of the wedding party, if only because he traditionally offers the very public best-man's toast (for details on all his duties—as well as the responsibilities of the rest of the wedding party—see Chapter 4.) Choosing this person can also be a touchy process, especially if you're equally close to two friends, two brothers, or a brother and a friend. If it comes down to the third scenario, it's wise to default to the blood-is-thicker-than-water theory and go with your brother. Your friend should understand. If dealing with the first two scenarios, however, you'll have to use some Kissinger-like diplomacy. But hey, you're getting married. You're a grown-up now; we know you can handle it.

When you've decided on who you'll ask to be best man, you'll of course have to get his buy-in, as well. To ask him, be as casual or as formal with your request as your personal style dictates—while some grooms will ask casually over the phone, others would rather bestow this honor by taking his brother/friend out to dinner or a sports event, or at the very least, wait until he sees him in person. There is no traditional etiquette on how to ask; the key is simply letting your best man know how much it will mean to you to have him by your side during this important time in your life.

Nuptial No-Nos

To avoid embarrassment, be sure to choose a best man you can rely upon to act maturely and mirror your best interests. In other words, don't choose a best man who is known for his violent outbursts, who detests your bride, who is in love with your bride, or who thinks marriage is a pointless, archaic institution.

Do Groomsmen Have to be Well-Groomed?

The same caveats for choosing a best man apply to picking your groomsmen. Choose close relatives and good friends only—guys you think you have a good chance of still knowing in ten years. It's nice to include your bride's brothers, but it's only necessary if you're close to them. However, if *not* including them will cause major family strife, you may wish to simply suck it up.

There are other alternatives as well. Your choices aren't limited to males only: one groom we know had a close girlfriend participate in his wedding party—and although she wore a bridesmaid dress, she was definitely included because of her friendship with the groom. The theory behind all your choices is to make this as smooth an operation as possible, without creating life-long enemies or injured egos.

While the groomsmen won't have quite as much responsibility as the best man, they will have some specific duties to fulfill (again, these are covered in Chapter 4).

 Groom Gambit

Choose among your more responsible, mature friends and family members to be groomsmen. You don't want to have to badger them to get fitted for formalwear or worry that they're sleeping off a bender on the morning of your wedding.

Other Honorary Positions

Suppose your bride enlists only four bridesmaids. She's insisting that your *attendants* equal hers in number, so that the wedding photos are "balanced." But you can't ask Richie without asking Potsie, Ralph, and Chachi—and your two brothers are *groomsmen*, too. What's a guy to do?

Your first choice is to compromise with the bride and have more groomsmen than bridesmaids. (Contrary to popular belief, this is perfectly acceptable.) If she simply won't agree to this option, however, you can avoid snubbing the other special people in your life by assigning some honorary tasks, such as reading passages during the ceremony, bringing gifts to the altar, or serving as extra *ushers*. Keep in mind that your bride might want to assign some of these positions, too, even if she *is* being unreasonable about the number of attendants. You can also be creative and make up new honorary positions; a male version of the "personal attendant" can help ensure that your socks match, your tie is on correctly, and your shaving nicks have stopped bleeding. A "bartender" can make sure the limo is stocked for the ride after the ceremony and can ride with you to the reception. (Think the Fonz.) It's your day: You and your bride can do what you want to make as many people as you choose a special part of the festivities.

Ask your clergyman about other honorary positions at the ceremony.

Wedding Words

What's the difference between **attendants, groomsmen, ushers,** and the best man? The best man is a special groomsman. The groomsmen act as ushers, seating people at the wedding and rolling out the runner for the bride to walk down. They're all considered attendants. You'll hear these terms used interchangeably throughout your wedding planning.

Choosing Clergy

When choosing clergy, you'll first need to decide with your bride where the ceremony will take place—in a church, temple, outdoors, and so on (or she'll decide for you). This choice may be a given if you've both belonged to the same church or temple your whole lives.

You then have the option of being married by the clergyperson serving that venue, or of asking a clergy member who's a relative or close family friend to do the honors. (Perhaps a close friend has entered the ministry, or you have an uncle or family friend who's a priest or rabbi.) You might not necessarily be able to substitute your clergy for the clergy in attendance at the site you choose, but you should weigh these options with your family. By the way—it's also appropriate to invite this clergy member to both the rehearsal dinner and the reception, where he or she can also give a special blessing.

If you're having a civil ceremony, the same rules apply. You will need to find someone legally authorized to perform the ceremony (a judge, a justice of the peace, even a notary public—this will vary by county, state, or country). Again, you may wish to personalize it by asking a friend or family member who has legal rights to perform the ceremony.

The Guest List

Ah, the guest list. It's the time you must decide, in writing, who makes the final friendship cut and who doesn't. It'll be there for all the world to see. Sound like fun?

The guest list is probably one of the most difficult things you will be responsible for when preparing for the wedding. There are never enough open spots, it seems, to fit in your family, childhood friends, high school friends, college friends, work pals, and golf buddies, without going into debt for life. Somehow, you'll have to finesse this list.

The best thing to do is to settle upon an unequivocal number of guests to invite—a number that you, your bride, and your families agree upon in advance. Depending on who's footing most of the bill, this could be wholly up to you, or you might be at the mercy of your bride and her family, who will give you a number to work with (usually around half the total guest list). You'll then need to talk to your parents about who they want to invite among their family and friends and, at the same time, coordinate your own list of friends and business associates. Unless your family is footing half the bill, it's rude for you—or them—to insist on inviting more people than the agreed-upon number.

 **Groom Gambit** _____

> If you and your bride are paying for the reception costs, it's up to you to decide how many people you'll invite. Work within your budget to figure out a final head count. Establish a number before you start creating your list, or things can quickly get out of hand.

Unless you have an unlimited budget, you'll probably have to make some tough choices when it comes to inviting guests. The nice thing about being the groom is that you can blame it on the bride's family if offended acquaintances question you; simply respond with, "Her family is throwing a small wedding." And you don't have to invite every person whose wedding you've attended in the past, especially if your wedding is going to be on the smaller side. People understand that weddings are an expensive proposition. If they act ungraciously, they really weren't good friends in the first place.

Guest-List Strategies

One strategy for inviting more people is this. If your parents are paying the reception costs, offer to pay for each extra person you want to invite above and beyond the guest count you've agreed upon. At a national average of about $50 a head for food and liquor, you might rethink inviting that freshman roommate you haven't talked to since graduating college or the guy in your office building who you talk hockey with every morning.

Nuptial No-Nos

When cutting names from your guest list, don't start with family. Traditional etiquette advises to cut business acquaintances first, then friends, and then family.

An additional option is inviting people without inviting their dates. Presumably, you'll invite established couples of whom you know both halves, but the theory is that if a friend or family member doesn't have a current squeeze, you invite him or her singly. This can be problematic if your buddy claims he's met the girl of his dreams a month before your wedding—especially if it's the seventh girl of his dreams since college, according to your calculations. It can be awkward deciding whose better half is "serious" enough to warrant inviting. But if you've got a few friends with absolutely no romantic entanglements, invite them alone. They might just get lucky with a single bridesmaid, anyway.

Be prepared to expect complaints even under the best of conditions—or at the very least, passive-aggressive response cards. We know of one Chicago guy who was invited alone but sent his response card indicating that "two" would be attending. This is just plain rude, of course, but you'll have to get used to major etiquette breaches; after all, not everyone has a book to guide their way.

On the other hand, don't be an etiquette buffoon yourself. Keep in mind that if you do adopt this strategy, you should be sensitive to the individual needs of your guests. If you know someone will be particularly uncomfortable if he or she comes without a date, then be sure to invite him or her *with* a date. The bottom line? Be sensitive to specific situations. After all, the point is for your guests to enjoy themselves—not view your wedding as an unwelcome obligation.

Give This Chapter to Your Best Man and Groomsmen

In This Chapter

- Traditional best-man duties
- The all-important best-man toast
- The bachelor party
- Traditional groomsmen duties

Not many men know exactly what's in store when they're asked to be best man or a groomsman at a friend's or family member's wedding—especially if this is his first time bestowed with such an honor. He'll probably need a little guidance on exactly what he's supposed to do—and *not* do. This chapter outlines, step-by-step, what each member of your party is responsible for, with tips to help them do it all in stride.

The Best Man Grand Plan

The role of best man is laden with responsibility. Perhaps it's because, unlike a woman's circle of supportive friends, men usually rely on each other for on-the-surface "support," like having a pal to shoot a few hoops with or get a beer with at a minute's notice. But being designated best man changes all that. With all the pressure and unfamiliar emotion of being a groom, your best man will need to go beyond the typical parameters of male friendship, providing an "assigned" shoulder to lean on throughout the engagement and wedding.

Typically, the best man is also much more high profile than the maid or matron of honor, if only because of the very public wedding-day toast he delivers. But the best man's duties don't start and end there. From a traditional standpoint, his duties begin the day he accepts this responsibility. This is one of the few times in life when a guy is going to need a real "best friend," in the true sense of the word, to alleviate the stress of planning, dealing with his bride and in-laws, and preparing for the holy sanctity of lifelong marriage.

Choose wisely. Don't choose your college drinking buddy who's always resented your fiancée for "taking you away from him." This combination has ugly engraved all over it. Don't choose your black-sheep brother just because you're related; the temptation might be too great for him to use your wedding as a public forum for his life-long grievances. (One best man we know got so drunk that during his speech, he actually began insulting the bride, his parents, and his brother (the groom). His father had to physically pull him off "stage," and it seemed like an eternity until the tension lifted.) You and your parents will spend a lot of time, money, and energy to plan this wedding; you don't want to ruin it with some ill-chosen clod as your best man.

What Does Your Best Man Do?

Here are the best man's traditional duties:

- Act as moral support through the engagement process.
- Plan and execute the bachelor party.
- Deliver the groom in a timely fashion to the wedding ceremony.
- Carry and protect the wedding bands.
- Stand next to the groom during the ceremony.
- Act as an official witness to the exchange, signing the wedding certificate.
- (Optional) Give the clergy a "donation" on behalf of the groom.
- Prepare and provide a well-formed speech prior to (or immediately following) the wedding repast (and optionally, at the rehearsal dinner).

Moral Support

As the groom, you may soon encounter some unfamiliar pressures. You've probably lived on your
own for a while now, and you're used to making
your own decisions and running your own life—
and now you are thrust into a situation in which
compromise takes the place of sheer independence.
Warning: Things may become stressful. And even if
it's stress you experience indirectly (your bride and
the maid of honor have a falling-out, your in-laws
are at each other's throats), chances are you'll hear
about every last stressful detail associated with this
wedding. Add that to any family, friend, or financial-
related pressures of your own to deal with.

Your best man should be your go-to guy to get away
from it all. Even if you're not the "talk-it-out" type,
your best man can provide moral support by being a
distraction in a storm of discontent.

Direct note to the best man: *Your goal is to provide
"moral support," not "immoral support." By providing
distractions, we don't mean encouraging the groom to join
you in picking up chicks or frequenting your favorite
strip club. As the best man, you're there to help solve the
groom's problems and challenges, not create new ones.*

*In addition, we encourage you to be positive about the
bride. Dissing her in front of the groom will do you no
good, and unless you have concrete evidence of a major
grievance (nothing short of murder or proven infidelity),
keep your mouth shut. Remember: Doing your best to get
along with the bride now will go a long way toward preserving your friendship with the groom in the future. If
she feels that you are undermining her, or that you don't*

have her best interests at heart, you will be sure to suffer the consequences in the long run. (Most happily married men will work harder to preserve domestic harmony than their relationships with drinking buddies.)

The Bachelor Party

Depending on the bride, the bachelor party will invoke different levels of distaste and distrust. No rational woman loves thinking about her guy reverting to Cro-Magnon man, getting as drunk as humanly possible while watching women in various stages of undress. Of course, you'll plead innocence because theoretically your best man is in charge; he's the one planning it, and you have to go along with whatever he's planned, right? Here's a hint: You're marrying your bride presumably because she's smarter than that. She's still going to hold you responsible for any misdeeds.

If you don't want the heat, make sure it's clear to your best man that he stays out of the kitchen. Or at the very least, that he makes sure what happens in the kitchen stays in the kitchen. You don't want a major blow-up the week before the wedding, as with one couple we know whose best man was called the morning after the bachelor party and told by the bride that he would no longer be a welcome part of the wedding. Reportedly, he arranged for some "activities" at the bachelor party that she found … well, distasteful. They managed to mend fences in the week leading up the wedding, but some residual hard feelings and injured egos remained. So tread carefully.

Direct note to the best man: Plan a bachelor party that suits the groom. In other words, don't use this as an opportunity to fulfill your own fantasies, especially if you think the groom may object. If he's not the Vegas type, don't plan a weekend away gambling. If he's never been a fan of camping, don't assume that he wants to start now. And if he's told you he'd rather not have female "entertainment" as part of the party, honor his wishes. Remember, this day is about him—not you.

Of course, if the groom does want to walk on the wild side, and you don't have an inkling (or the inclination) on how to fulfill his every bachelor wish, you've got another problem. In this scenario, you may wish to involve a more willing groomsman to make the "arrangements." In other words, you don't need to compromise your own morals or feelings to appeal to the groom's every hedonistic fantasy.

We discuss more about bachelor parties in Chapter 7.

Best-Man Wedding-Day Duties

On the day of the wedding, tensions will be high. Your best man will help diffuse some of this stress by taking on certain responsibilities. First, he should help ensure that you're ready on time, and arrange for you to be delivered to the ceremony. Second, he is responsible for holding and producing the rings at the appropriate time during the ceremony. And third, he will literally be your right-hand man, standing next to you as you exchange vows during the ceremony. He should also be accessible for photos and wedding-party traditions throughout the reception.

Direct note to the best man: *By "best man" we stress the term "man." That means acting responsibly and maturely, especially the day of the wedding. In other words, don't pull a Vince Vaughn–inspired "Old School" stunt, like coughing out unsavory messages to the groom throughout the ceremony. Your audience, in this case, won't find it funny.*

 Groom Gambit

Remind your best man that the wedding reception includes more than his Gen-X buddies. He should tailor his speech to also appeal to the children, grandmas, and pregnant women in the room. Meaning, no limericks or off-color jokes— or unseemly references to the bachelor party.

Tips for the Best Man's Toast

We've heard some great speeches and some truly awful, awkward, uncomfortable ones. The person you choose as best man may not be a natural orator, but at least instill in him (or have one of the groomsmen instill in him) the importance of a little preparation beforehand. Whether he writes out some notes, practices in front of a mirror, or memorizes the entire thing, a good speech from the best man adds class and requisite sentimentality to your wedding.

Here are some tips to share with your best man. They're also useful for your own speech, if you choose to deliver one. As the groom, you can say a few words at the rehearsal dinner—as a toast preceding dinner, for example—or at an appropriate time during the reception.

- **Keep it simple.** For the less-experienced speaker, keeping it short and sweet will make a speech easier to deliver and easier for the audience to follow and enjoy. Long, drawn-out anecdotes and complicated jokes should be avoided.

- **Do your homework.** Include anecdotes that are funny, flattering, or from the heart. Avoid clichés and generic-sounding toasts. Kept in good taste, a personal speech makes an audience more interested and receptive.

- **Write it down.** No one will fault you for subtly referring to index cards.

- **Practice.** Rehearse the speech with a friend or your dog.

- **Don't drown your fears.** One drink may calm your nerves, but five might make you incoherent. Lay off the booze until *after* the speech.

- **Get training.** Now might be the perfect time to take a class in public speaking, such as the popular Dale Carnegie series. It may seem like overkill for a relatively short wedding toast, but you'll develop skills you can use for life.

What About the Groomsmen?

The groomsmen do not have quite as much responsibility as the best man, but they should be counted on for a number of traditional duties. Here they are:

- Provide moral support during the engagement.
- Attend pre-wedding events.
- Acquire or rent the proper wedding-day attire.
- Arrive on time at the ceremony site.
- Usher guests to their seats.
- Sit at the reception bridal table.
- Endure the long photography session (with you!).

Moral Support

Direct note to groomsmen: See section on the difference between "moral" and "immoral" support, detailed earlier in this chapter for the best man.

Attend Pre-Wedding Events

The groomsmen should be invited to all major pre-wedding events, including the engagement party, any "Jack-and-Jill" showers, the bachelor party, and the rehearsal and rehearsal dinner. They should do their best to attend as many as possible. If they live out of town, be sure to give them plenty of notice about planned events—and if they can't make all of them, try to be understanding. However, they should make a good-faith effort to attend as many events as they are invited to. In addition, groomsmen may wish to prepare a few words to offer at the rehearsal dinner, during which multiple toasts are traditionally offered.

Direct note to groomsmen: *If you are issued an invitation for a wedding-related party, be sure to RSVP by the date noted on the invitation, indicating whether or not you can make it (and whether you're bringing a guest, if one is invited). The party planners will need a proper head count to organize the event, and nothing is more annoying than tracking down non-RSVPers. Equally important—if you RSVP "yes," be sure to show up unless there is an unavoidable emergency or conflict. For many events, your presence is paid for in advance by those planning the party. This makes it especially inconsiderate if you're a no-show.*

Groom Gambit

Be sure your groomsmen (and best man, for that matter) know exactly where they need to be and at what time for all pre-wedding and wedding-day events. Also be sure to give them a heads-up on their specific responsibilities, as they're probably relatively clueless about wedding traditions. A wedding rehearsal is a great time to go through these duties, but if that's not possible be sure to send each groomsman a detailed itinerary so there are no surprises (or lame excuses!).

Wedding-Day Duties

On the day of the wedding itself, your grooms-men have a few key duties, the most important of which is arriving on time and in order. (This means wearing the proper attire—clean and pressed—as dictated by the groom.) At the ceremony, grooms-men are in charge of seating guests (bride's family and friends on the left, groom's family and friends on the right) as well as distributing wedding-day programs. All the while, you'll be sweating it out with little to do besides squirm in the back as you wait for the wedding to begin ....

At the reception, groomsmen may be asked to take part in certain traditions, such as walking in when they're announced to guests, dancing with bridesmaids to a designated song, sitting at the "head table" if you choose to have one, and participating in the seemingly endless photo session. One idea, especially if you have easily distracted groomsmen or a large wedding party, is to offer everyone a pre-printed wedding-day agenda so that all participants know exactly when they'll need to be on their toes.

Direct note to groomsmen: *On the wedding day, it is important to be accountable. Do not disappear at any point during the wedding, as you may be needed for pictures, a special dance, or other wedding-party duties. (One groomsman we know went to take a nap in his car after imbibing one too many during the cocktail hour. This type of behavior obviously should be avoided.)*

Chapter 5

Let the Games Begin: Planning the Details

In This Chapter

- Choosing the ceremony and reception sites
- What to look for in a photographer
- Choosing your music
- Special transportation
- Girl stuff—flowers, stationery, and the bridal registry

So your pre-game plan is complete—you've got your budget, you've got your best man, you've got your groomsmen—and you've *already* got a headache. Depending on how things have gone so far, you're aware of just how much more you're going to get involved in the party planning. Your bride and her mother may have everything totally under control—and that's okay with you. Or you might find you like putting in your two cents—especially if you're contributing a lot more than that to the budget. Whatever the case, this chapter is an overview of some of the specific elements that will need addressing well before your wedding day, with a special emphasis on the stuff you care more about.

Get Me to the Church (or Chuppah) on Time

If you and your bride met in church, choosing the site of your ceremony is easy. Chances of that are probably slim, however, so there's bound to be some debate, even if you share the same faith. If you have two different faiths, live far away from your hometowns, or practice no religion, the question becomes even more complicated. Traditionally, the bride and her family chose the wedding site because they were footing the bill. But if that's not the case, if you feel strongly about this issue, or if you want to choose something a bit more unusual, you've got some options:

Traditional wedding sites ...

- The college chapel of your alma mater
- The church or temple you've attended all your life
- The church or temple you've joined together
- The stunning church or temple your bride has always dreamed of marrying in
- Your reception site—a room adjacent to the hotel ballroom or the garden outside the reception hall

- A public park
- Your own home or a relative's

Creative wedding sites ...

- A yacht
- A ballpark
- A museum or art gallery
- Under a beautiful tent on your rich uncle's estate
- A hot-air balloon
- Under water
- The beach
- The slopes
- The golf course

One unforgettable wedding we attended was in an intimate, open-air theater, with a reception following in a beautifully appointed barn with white-washed walls, formal table settings, and candlelight. The rustic yet semiformal décor lent the wedding a completely unique atmosphere.

Interfaith Ceremonies

You're Catholic, she's Jewish. If you thought you could only have a civil ceremony (to the dismay of one or both of your families), you're wrong. With any luck, one of the following options will calm even the most irate family member:

- Combine both faiths with co-officiating clergy. If your clergy is reluctant to (or simply won't) participate, seek out college chaplains or more liberal-minded clergy in your area.

- Turn to a tolerant third religion, such as the Unitarian Church, which encourages couples to structure services that reflect both religions.

- Choose one religion over the other in which to conduct your ceremony.

- Plan two wedding ceremonies, one in each faith. (One could take place on a day separate from your reception day, if necessary.)

Groom Gambit

Planning the ceremony can be the most sensitive issue of your wedding. Even laissez-faire parents can become incensed if you plan something nontraditional. Prepare in advance for opposition to proposed plans, especially if your parents or grandparents are devoutly religious and you're marrying outside the faith.

Party Time

So you've gotten through planning the ceremony, without offending too many people. Now, it's time to plan the fun part—the reception. Contrary to popular belief, there are many kinds of receptions, so it's up to you to choose what style, length, and level of formality you prefer. You might want to consolidate the ceremony and reception site at one location so guests won't have to travel or kill time in between. Or if that's not an option, have the ceremony and reception in separate locations. No matter what you choose, allow it to be a reflection of your—and your bride's—personal style.

Depending on your budget and preferences, you have a number of choices. For a more subdued, shorter affair with limited expenses, you may choose to have a daytime garden-style cake-and-punch reception, where there is no formal meal served. Or if you prefer an evening occasion, host an hors d'oeuvres reception with a limited bar. If you choose either of these options, be sure that guests know ahead of time; at the majority of today's weddings, guests expect a full meal. You don't want them starving and cranky when they find out there's only light finger food at your reception.

Nuptial No-Nos

If you're having a reception with a limited meal or no meal, be sure that guests know ahead of time. Most guests assume they will be fed at a wedding reception and may be upset if they come to your wedding hungry.

More elaborate, traditional receptions feature full meals. You can choose either buffet or sit-down-style meals, depending on your preferences. *Food-station receptions*, a variation of the traditional buffet, have also become popular. A food-station reception consists of a collection of small buffet or grazing areas, set out in separate areas of the room. Each area features a different type of food, and may include more contemporary fare such as stir-fry, fajitas, or sushi, in addition to traditional carving stations of turkey or roast beef. You can also offer a dessert station, such as an ice-cream-sundae bar or a pastry bar, to end the evening on a sweet note.

Wedding Words

Food-station receptions are typically like cocktail parties—less structured, with a bar that generally stays open all evening and no defined place settings or assigned table. Just don't forget to eat!

Sit-down dinners can range from a formal, five-course meal to a less-formal meal with fewer courses. Your style will depend on local custom, budget, and personal preference.

Of course, you can also forgo the traditional dinner reception in favor of a beach barbecue, park picnic, or a day at the ballpark. Guests might find it a refreshing change, and you might find that it's more relaxed and suited to your personalities.

Smile—You're Far from Candid Camera

For many grooms, the photography session can be a real drag. You're forced to stand stiffly, sweating in your formalwear for an exorbitant amount of time while your friends are just a spitting distance away, enjoying cocktails and regaling each other with old college stories. Hey, isn't this *your* wedding day? Come to think of it, do you really even want these pictures anyway?

Once your wedding day is history and all you have are fond but dim memories, you will appreciate your wedding photos. Actually, you'll probably even want some kind of say in choosing a photographer so that you don't end up with some guy or gal who's at best condescending and at worst downright irritating.

Nuptial No-Nos

It may be tempting to choose a friend or other amateur to take your wedding photos to save money, but don't leave such important photographs to chance. You've only got one shot to preserve these once-in-a-lifetime moments.

Here are some things to consider when choosing a photographer:

- Choose a professional with solid experience, top-of-the line equipment, and good lighting who will efficiently guide your group to pose for all appropriate photos. Ask friends, your caterer, and parents for referrals, and view samples of the photographer's previous work before you book him or her.

- Take some posed shots so that you're sure to include all close family members, the wedding party, and as many guests as possible.

- Encourage candid shots, or choose a photographer who specializes in photo-journalistic style, catching spontaneous and emotional moments rather than only posed, formal shots.

- Place portable cameras on each table for guests to photograph each other.

- Be sure to get a signed contract with the details on cost and the amount of time the photographer will spend at the wedding.

When and if you also choose a videographer, use the same tips and beware of any additional editing or creative costs you might incur, based on the videographer's style.

The Wedding Singer

You saw the movie. A guy with a bad voice and a mullet haircut sings hot tunes from the '80s and woos Drew Barrymore. Now it's your turn to find similar entertainment for your shindig. Warning: Although this movie was a sentimental look back at another decade, there are still guys out there doing weddings who look and sing like Adam Sandler's character (without Adam's movie-star appeal).

Our point? Choose your music carefully, whether it's live or not. Make sure you've had a chance to see your musicians or DJ in action ahead of time. And think twice about taking your parents' band recommendations as gospel. Then again, they might just know something about music that transcends time and generations. Just be sure to check out the band in question ahead of time.

The same goes for a DJ. We've all been to a wedding or two where the DJ makes himself the star of the show in favor of the music he's supposed to be playing. The worst of these DJs may crack bad jokes or create irritating games for guests to play. Don't let some frustrated performer make your wedding his personal stage—unless, of course, you like bad jokes and irritating games. Here are some other things to remember:

- When choosing a band or DJ, it's best to start with referrals from friends and family.

- Think carefully before employing your cousin's garage band just to save some cash. Chances are, your guests won't like them quite as much as you do, and a wedding is a serious first gig for cousin Eddie to play.

- Sometimes, a band can vary its number of performers. If this is the case, consider having fewer band members to save some money. Be sure to listen to the scaled-down version before you book them, however.

- Check with the band to see whether they provide a sound system to continue the music when they're taking breaks.

- When using a DJ, create a list of songs you'd like to hear and give it to him or her before the day of your wedding.

- If you'd like the DJ or bandleader to introduce your wedding party or perform other announcements, give this information to him or her—in writing—ahead of time.

- Be sure to get the contract details in writing, including the cost, the amount of time they'll perform, and what type of restitution you'll get if they cancel. (It's been known to happen.)

Groom Gambit _____

Don't forget to give your band or DJ a list of songs to play during special dances such as the mother/son, father/daughter, and couple's first dance. First dance songs can come from any era or genre—choose your personal favorite or go with a classic standard.

Ceremony and Cocktail-Hour Music

Aside from your after-dinner dance music, you'll also need to choose music for your ceremony and cocktail hour. (Dead air has been known to kill the party.)

For your ceremony, you'll want to speak with the music director at your church, temple, or ceremony site. He or she has done this many times before and will have a good idea of what you'll need. There are more options besides the traditional wedding march when your bride walks down the aisle, and music can be incorporated to be a large part of the ceremony. Oftentimes you're obligated to use the ceremony site's own singer or musicians; beware of this contingency, especially if you're not fond of their style.

For your cocktail hour, you've got some options. You may wish to hire some separate musicians to play, such as a string quartet, piano player, or harpist. One wedding we attended featured a strolling violinist during dinner, who would play guests' requests. Another featured a steel-drum band at an outdoor cocktail hour. Of course, it might be cost-prohibitive to hire two groups of live musicians, so talk to your caterer or reception-site manager to find out whether they have any other options, such as a built-in sound system with which you can pipe in satellite music or your own CD creations.

Wheels

So you've always wanted to ride in an antique Rolls? Or a stretch Lincoln Navigator with the works? Now's your chance (and possibly the only time your new wife will agree to such automotive extravagances). On your wedding day, you might not want to worry about driving yourself around. And you'll probably want to ride to your reception with the traveling party who are your groomsmen and bridesmaids. Between the stress of the wedding, a couple of drinks, and a long day, either designate someone as the day's or evening's driver, or hire a chauffeur. If you prefer to use your own car, take advantage of the "getaway" car tradition, whereby the ushers "decorate" your car during the reception. This is a quaint and, in our opinion, sadly forgotten tradition.

Groom Gambit

Check out the exteriors and interiors of the cars you'll be hiring to make sure they're in good shape and can seat the proper number of people.

If you do hire limousines or other cars, be sure to remember a few things:

- Book it six months ahead of time.

- Comparison-shop for the best price.

- Be sure the company is a licensed, above-board operation. Check with the Better Business Bureau or only hire from referrals.

- Meet the driver, and choose your specific car ahead of time. If you don't, you may end up with a different color or model than you expected. Specify it in the contract.

- Be sure to provide the proper information to the company ahead of time, including pick-up locations, times, and whether the cars should wait between each destination.

- Find out about recourse if your hired car breaks down or it isn't the one you agreed to in the contract.

Girl Stuff

Other components involved in planning a wedding include choosing flowers, stationery, and church and reception decorations. Unless you have a keen design sense (or you have reservations about your intended's taste), you probably won't want to be overly involved in these decisions. The following outlines strictly the basics.

Flowers

Flowers are expensive. If you're contributing financially to your wedding, don't underestimate the cost of fresh blooms. Obviously, costs will vary, depending on whether you choose centerpieces of tropical flora on every table or simple bowls of wildflowers. Plan to spend more than you'd likely ever estimate.

Stationery

Stationery necessities include the invitation itself, the inserts regarding reception information, the reply card, and another stamped envelope. You will also need to budget for place cards, thank-you cards, and a *wedding program* (which is optional).

One groom, a writer from Buffalo, NY, fashioned his wedding program into a playbill entitled "Til Death Do Us Part," by "Jack and Mary Productions." Inside were fun profiles on the "cast members," as well as the bride and groom's "story"—the history of how they met. It made guests feel more personally involved in the wedding.

Wedding Words

A **wedding program** contains information about the ceremony readings and music, as well as such fun reading as wedding attendant profiles. The program can be customized as creatively as you'd like.

Stationery can also be expensive, especially if you're printing a lot of invitations or are using more extravagant touches like high-end paper or engraving. A great way to save money—and choose from a huge selection—is to purchase invitations online; simply do a search for "wedding invitations," and observe as thousands of related pages pop up on your screen. It's easier than flipping through the Yellow Pages ....

Decorations

Leave the decorating to your bride and her mother. I promise you won't regret it—unless their taste is so god-awful or ostentatious that you find it absolutely necessary to interject. But you wouldn't be marrying a woman with bad taste, anyway, would you?

But be warned. If you offer up an opinion on every little thing, your fiancée will then likely assume you want to be included in every maddening detail of the wedding. Of course, if you do decide to wash your hands of something, such as flowers, then stick with it. Don't jump in at the eleventh hour with some random, unwelcome opinion like, "I hate posies."

Traditional Duties of the Groom

In this chapter we've covered a lot of wedding-related planning. Of course, there's a chance that the only thing you want to be involved in wedding-wise is what you absolutely, positively have no way of avoiding. In other words, you want to follow the dictates of traditional etiquette—which involves much less responsibility than what's implied in this book. If this is the case, we think the following section alone justifies the price of this book—if only because it will enable you to do the minimal number of allowable tasks leading up to your wedding.

Timeline of duties traditionally assigned the groom:

Six months before the wedding ...

- Decide the division of financial obligations.
- Set a budget.
- Set an appointment with the clergy.
- Prepare your guest list.

- Choose your best man and ushers.
- Plan your honeymoon.
- Check passports and visas.

Four months before the wedding …

- Buy wedding rings and order engraving.
- Select formalwear.
- Find a new place to live. (Yes, you will have to abandon roommates Brendan and Rodney forever.)
- Shop for new home furnishings (or start begging family members for giveaways).
- Make reservations for the honeymoon.
- Coordinate lodging options for out-of-town guests.
- Have a complete physical exam and update your immunizations.
- Set an appointment for the blood test (if applicable in your state).

Two months …

- Set a date with your fiancée to get the marriage license.

One month …

- Make reservations for the rehearsal dinner.
- Select your bride's gift and gifts for the attendants.

- Review legal, medical, and church documents.
- Confirm honeymoon details and reservations.

Two weeks ...

- Move belongings to your new home.
- Have a bachelor party or dinner.

One week ...

- Confirm the time and place of the wedding rehearsal and rehearsal dinner with all the attendants.
- Give the final guest count to the rehearsal dinner restaurant.
- Pick up wedding rings.
- Pick up your formalwear.
- Give the best man the clergy's fee in a sealed envelope for delivery.
- Pack for the honeymoon.

Whew, that still seems like a lot, doesn't it? But that doesn't even touch upon any of the actual party-planning aspects, such as the reception, music, flowers, stationery ... the list goes on. Consider how lucky you are to be male, and think of how proud and happy your bride will be if you actually complete these tasks without being asked a minimum of three times first.

Chapter 6

Alternative Weddings: Getting Creative

In This Chapter

- What's a theme wedding?
- Theme-wedding ideas
- Destination wedding how-tos
- Ethnic weddings
- Creative touches

If you think you're stuck with the standard, by-the-book wedding similar to the six you attended last year alone, think again. More and more brides and grooms are getting creative—making their weddings more interesting and memorable for themselves and for their guests. Little touches can go a long way, and weddings are also growing more reflective of the bride's and groom's personalities. From the ceremony to the send-off, couples are finding new ways to put their own personal stamp on their celebrations. These unique touches can range from full-scale theme weddings, such as

Medieval or Fairy-Tale weddings, to highly personal wedding favors, menus, or music within the standard conventions of the wedding celebration.

What's in a Theme?

So what is a *theme wedding*, anyway? Theme weddings are full-blown extravaganzas that revolve around one dominant idea or concept. More popular theme weddings in recent years include Medieval/Renaissance, Victorian, Roaring Twenties, and Fairy Tale/Cinderella themes. These weddings are generally characterized by elaborate costumes, accessories, and decor representing the time period, special menus, a theme-wedding cake, creative transportation, era-specific music, and so on.

Theme weddings can also include wackier ideas such as underwater weddings and hot-air balloon weddings, or holiday-inspired weddings held on special days ranging from Halloween to New Year's Eve to the Fourth of July.

Wedding Words

A **theme wedding** is any wedding that has an overriding concept behind it, to which your wedding traditions—such as your ceremony, food, and cake—adhere.

Basically, a theme wedding is anything your creativity dictates it to be. There are no parameters limiting you—aside from your imagination, of course.

Why Have a Theme Wedding?

There are countless reasons to throw a theme wedding, most of which are highly personal to you and your bride. You may be tired of attending one similar wedding after the next, and crave something different for your own fete. Or you may share a passion for a hobby, sport, or time in history that you'd love to incorporate into one the most important days of your life. No matter what the reason, a theme wedding can provide an interesting backdrop and special touches that your guests will never forget.

Nuptial No-Nos

If you're going to plan an alternative wedding, don't mix themes. Guests will be impressed by a well-carried-out concept—but just plain confused by a mish-mash of random ideas.

A theme wedding also provides a great way for you, the groom, to get more involved in the planning—and have a lot more fun. After all, finding a vintage 1920s Model T to rent and a twenties-style orchestra (for a Roaring Twenties wedding) will be a lot more fun than registering for china and choosing corsages. In other words, with a theme wedding, your skills will be put to use in a much more appropriate manner—with a much more satisfying payoff in the end.

What's a Good Theme?

A good theme can incorporate anything you have an interest or passion for. If you met your bride golfing and you both share a love of the sport, for instance, a golf course may be the perfect venue for your ceremony. If you're wilderness aficionados, have guests hike to your ceremony under a forest canopy. If you love wine, throw your wedding at a vineyard, and feature wine-tasting as part of the entertainment. Huge science-fiction fans? Throw a futuristic wedding with fun décor, outfits, and futuristic concept cars transporting you from place to place. The point is, your possibilities are limitless—it's up to you to explore where your interests lie and what type of party you'd like to throw.

Theme-Wedding Ideas

So you'd like to have a theme wedding but the perfect idea's not instantly popping to mind? The following are some themes to consider:

- **Country-western wedding.** Feature square-dancing for entertainment (hire an instructor), wear cowboy hats and boots, and serve a mouth-watering barbecue.

- **Reggae wedding.** Serve tropical drinks and Caribbean food, invite guests in beachwear, and hire a steel-drum band.

- **"Great beyond" wedding.** Hold your reception in a planetarium. Use silver and black for your wedding colors and play techno music.

- **Winery wedding.** Choose a vineyard or winery for the venue, hold a formal wine-tasting with all the trappings, and give fancy wine corks for wedding favors.

- **Sports-related.** Hold your ceremony on the field/court, design the wedding cake to look like sports equipment, have big-screen TVs with greatest sports highlights playing.

- **Ski wedding.** Marry at the top of the mountain, ski down, and party afterward in the chalet.

- **Medieval wedding.** Choose a Renaissance fairgrounds as your site, rent or purchase period costumes, and serve mead, wine, and turkey legs—no utensils necessary.

- **Victorian wedding.** Choose a period inn or home as your venue, don the clothing of the era, serve lots of tea and sweets.

- **Disco wedding.** Find a great dance club, an even better DJ, and some retro threads for the dance party of the year.

- **Safari wedding.** Dress in safari garb, decorate with old steamer trunks and mosquito netting, and have a pig and ox roast.

- **Roaring Twenties wedding.** Dress in classic tuxes and flapper-wear, play great '20s pop tunes, and throw a Gatsby-esque affair.
- **Marathon wedding.** Hold your ceremony at the beginning—or the end—of the race. (Might make you get there that much faster.)

Holiday Wedding Ideas

Of course, you can also take advantage of the holiday spirit to inspire your celebration. Wrap your wedding around any holiday for an unusual and unforgettable celebration. Here are some possibilities:

- **Valentine's Day wedding.** Serve heart-shaped food. Give chocolate favors. Design your invitation to look like an old-fashioned Valentine. Decorate in red, pink, and white.
- **Fourth-of-July wedding.** Have an outdoor barbecue. Use red, white, and blue for your decorating theme. Shoot off fireworks after dark. Give sparklers as wedding favors.
- **Thanksgiving wedding.** Have a truly elaborate Turkey feast, or recreate the pilgrims' first dinner. Use gourds and squashes for centerpieces. Give wish-bones to every couple as favors.

- **Halloween wedding.** Wear black (you *and* the bride). Choose a gothic venue, like an old church or castle. Set up traditional diversions for the kids, such as a haunted house and bobbing for apples. Give little bags of candy as favors (no tricks!).

- **Christmas wedding.** Pick a venue that's already decorated (and save on flowers, etc.). Wear a velvet bow tie and cummerbund. Give little gift-wrapped favors to guests. Have Santa pay a visit and distribute guest "gifts."

- **New Year's wedding.** Begin the reception *before* the ceremony—then get married at midnight. Serve lots of champagne. Make it black-tie only. Party 'til the wee hours.

Destination Weddings

Another type of alternative wedding is the destination wedding, first referred to in Chapter 2. A destination wedding is when you, your bride, and select family and friends travel elsewhere to tie the knot—and celebrate afterward. The destination wedding is ideal if you'd like to have a somewhat private wedding in an exotic locale. It's also a great alternative if a traditional wedding just isn't your style. Think of it as a cross between eloping and a full-blown wedding. An even better feature of the destination wedding? Instant honeymoon.

Because they've grown in popularity in recent years, destination weddings are easier to plan than ever, though there can be some complications depending on your location. If you're marrying out of the country, for instance, be sure to learn about local wedding ordinances and guidelines as you plan your ceremony. Some countries require very specific forms of ID, or a wedding license, before a legal ceremony can take place.

Obviously, you will have planned the ceremony and reception before you get to your destination, unless you're planning an extended stay before your wedding date. If you're going to stay at a resort, you're probably in luck—many international resorts will offer help in planning from afar, and they may even have a professional wedding planner on staff. In areas like the Caribbean or Hawaii— extremely popular destination-wedding locations— you are almost assured of such service at the better hotels and resorts. Of course, you may also choose to hire an independent wedding coordinator to help with the details. Shop around on the Internet, or consult with a travel agent for specific recommendations. Be sure to check references and negotiate a contract with a wedding coordinator beforehand.

Groom Gambit

If you'd like your destination wedding to go as smoothly and easily as possible, choose a hotel or resort that has wedding planners on staff—as well as plenty of experience with prior weddings.

Ethnic Weddings

Another great way to personalize your wedding is to incorporate your ethnic heritage. Obviously, this is easiest if you and the bride both hail from the same place or share the same religion. But throwing an ethnic wedding can be just as doable—and even more interesting—if you and your bride come from different backgrounds. Instead of ignoring these differences, embrace them—and expose your guests, too, to the cultures and heritage that you'll both share once you're married.

If you are not already familiar with your ancestry's wedding traditions, talk to both sets of parents. Surely they will be honored that you wish to carry on—or bring back—traditions from your background. Tell them that you plan to honor both your cultures in various ways. For instance, if you are Italian and your fiancée is Indian, you may wish to serve Indian and Italian dishes, play both Italian and Indian music, and/or dress in Indian attire. You may even decide to hold two ceremonies if you wish to maintain the full integrity of your two religions or cultures—these may be held consecutively, one immediately following the first. Or you may wish to make a weekend out of it and hold one ceremony and reception the first day, and the other ceremony and reception the next day. If you choose to hold your celebrations on two consecutive days, you'll be able to honor all the traditions and practices of each of your backgrounds to their full extent, from ceremony rituals to music to the reception menu.

There are many ways you can incorporate cultural influences into your wedding, including the following:

- Pre-ceremony rituals
- Ceremonial customs
- Cultural clothing
- Jewelry
- Make-up or adornments
- Ethnic music
- Flowers
- Regional menus
- Ethnic-influenced decorating
- Favors that reflect your cultural background(s)
- Customized wedding cake
- Culturally relevant dances/entertainment

Making It Personal

Another way to add some pizzazz to your celebration—without throwing a full-blown theme wedding—is to personalize different aspects of it. That means taking your own personal interests and weaving them into the fabric of your wedding celebration. For instance, one sports-car-collecting groom in the Midwest put die-cast miniature sports cars at each table setting; a writer from New York City gave each guest a personalized, handmade bookmark with a few words he wrote himself. Personalizing your wedding in creative ways can enable your guests to feel more connected to you as a couple, and understand what makes one or both of you tick.

There's no end to the opportunities for adding personalized touches to your wedding. If you are a musician, write a special song for your bride to be performed at your ceremony—or with your band at the wedding. If your passion is riding, make an entrance at your ceremony on horseback. If you love music, custom-burn CDs you'd like played at your wedding—and give them as wedding favors to your guests. Even if your interest or profession is less obvious—you're a geologist, for instance—you can still reflect it in your wedding day: in this case, use interesting rock or mineral samples you've found over the years to create unforgettable centerpieces. The key is to tap into your interests and think creatively about how you can include them to best connect with your wedding guests.

No matter how you put your personal stamp onto your wedding festivities, it's sure to be remembered. And whether you go with a full-scale theme wedding or a more traditional wedding with some special, personal touches, your guests will undoubtedly feel more connected to you as a couple—and enjoy the fun and surprises along the way.

Chapter 7

Fluctuating Emotions: And You Thought Once a Month Was Bad

In This Chapter

- Holding on to your sanity
- Same-planet communication strategies
- She says/she means
- Inter-family communications
- Preparing for some major life changes

When you proposed, you made her a very happy woman—congratulations. Hold on to that elation because the most ironic part of weddings is that in preparing for the happiest day of her life, she might experience some of the worst—or at least the most pressure-filled—days. Conflicting opinions, unexpected situations, demanding in-laws, time pressures—any number of situations can combine to heighten her stress, and thus yours, by extension. Not to mention that you've just made one of the most important decisions of your life, so you might be a little further from carefree than you're used to. But there's hope: plenty of lesser men have gone through it before you. This chapter is your personal troubleshooting guide to getting through the rough spots. *Without* shooting yourself in the foot.

You Are a Rock

As you've probably deduced by now, planning a wedding is no easy task. Even if your fiancée is an event planner by profession, she's going to experience stress from planning this party. The reason? They are many and varied, but the gist of it is the cult of weddings: This is supposed to be the happiest day of her life, full of good weather, great food, and wonderful friends and family who all get along perfectly. Already it's easy to see where disappointment and frustration loom.

Chances are she's probably handling more of the details than you are in planning this event. If you got off lucky and you don't have to handle much outside the traditional groom stuff, here's your chance to shine. Be the man she's always dreamed of. Be her rock.

How to Be a Rock

It's hard to explain how to be a rock in a few simple words. It's more a way of life, a way of thinking, best described by personal anecdotes. The following are some real-life wedding horror stories and how these grooms of stone helped handle them:

- One Connecticut bride came down with Lyme disease three months before her wedding. Although the majority of planning was complete, the remaining pre-wedding tasks included fitting the dress, picking up stationery, meeting with musicians, meeting with the caterer, choosing and picking up favors, and so on. She was bedridden for two full weeks and still weak for a long time afterward—but her groom came to the rescue, running the errands she was unable to, helping address invitations, putting together favors, and meeting with the caterer. He even convinced the tailor to come to her house for her first fitting. Her friends and family were duly impressed.

- One bride in San Francisco nearly had a nervous breakdown when her band called a month before the wedding to cancel. At that short notice, she thought she'd never get a decent replacement for the wedding. The groom took matters into his own hands, calling on a friend who was currently touring with a band just on the verge of making it big. The band's days of performing venues like weddings were long over, but the groom managed to convince his friend and the band to make this one last wedding appearance. It cost him a little cash, and it wasn't necessarily traditional wedding music, but the rewards far out-weighed the cost when he saw how pleased his bride was—and how excited the guests were to have their own private concert.

● When one Minnesota bride was laid off from her high-profile chef's position a few weeks before her wedding, she was under-standably crushed to have to worry about getting a new job when all she wanted to think about was her upcoming wedding. Her groom convinced her to take this opportunity to start the catering business she had always dreamed about—and to put off worrying about it until *after* the wed-ding. He even offered to back her financially and support the two of them until she got her business off the ground.

The moral of the story? When things go wrong, it's your time to look good. As they say, take the ball and run with it.

Same-Planet Communication Strategies

If you've dated for a while, chances are you and your bride have had at least a few disagreements and have developed a basic pattern of working through them. You cannot underestimate the value of good communication in the pursuit of a strong marriage, especially when dealing with disagreements or conflicting interests. The engagement period is as good a time as any to brush up on these skills, especially because it's often rife with disagreements and conflicting interests. We describe the basic elements of "active listening" or "mirroring," a proven method of healthy, *constructive communication*.

 Wedding Words _____

The techniques that contribute to **constructive communication** in this section come from the experts at the Relationship Institute. You can find more information about the Relationship Institute at www.relationship-institute.com or by calling 248-546-0407.

The four major blocks to healthy communication that couples adopt in their interactions are

1. Arguing or withdrawing
2. Blaming and accusing
3. Not listening
4. Changing the subject

By using these blocks to good communication, a couple virtually ensures that they will not be able to resolve conflicts. Suppose you have plans to take your fiancée to dinner, and at 4:00 your best friend calls to offer a free ticket to the basketball game.

To you, it's a no-brainer: You've gotta go to the b-ball game, which was sold out weeks ago. But your fiancée isn't going to be happy, and you know that ahead of time. Such a situation requires finesse, and the following sections present some strategies to help you avoid major conflict.

Setting the Stage for Healthy Communication

For good communication to occur, you must choose the right time and place. If either of you is too upset or distracted, one of the four communication blocks will most likely end up hindering the discussion.

If you or your bride is too upset to have a constructive conversation, do the following:

1. Stop and cool down; leave the situation for a while, if necessary.
2. Set a specific time and place to talk again.
3. Don't interrupt her; let her finish her thoughts.
4. Acknowledge her concerns.

Using "I" Messages

Instead of blaming or accusing—starting sentences with "you always" or "you never"—it's best to take responsibility for what you're feeling and communicate it to your fiancée. If you begin your sentences with "I feel" or "I think," she'll be less likely to immediately jump to the defensive.

To put this strategy into action ...

1. Discuss your feelings in a responsible way.
2. If you discuss your fiancée's behavior, do so in terms of your feelings.
3. Let your fiancée know your feelings when she engages in the behavior—not three weeks later
4. Tell her the consequences of her behavior to you.

For instance, if you're upset when she doesn't call to tell you when she's coming home late, your first instinct might be to blame and accuse, saying, "You're irresponsible," "You don't care about me," or "You're selfish." Using "I" statements, the same statement might come out like this: "When you're late and you don't call, I feel hurt, frustrated, and angry. And when I'm hurt and angry, I don't feel like spending time with you."

Using Active Listening

With active listening, the listener's job is strictly to listen, without interruption and without adding anything to what the speaker has said.

The key elements of active listening are to ...

- **Listen to understand.** Even if you don't agree with what your fiancée is saying, pay attention and listen to it.
- **Summarize.** After you've heard her, paraphrase and repeat what you heard. "So what I heard you say was ...."

- **Verify.** When you're done summarizing what you heard, ask her, "Did I hear you correctly?" Let her give you feedback. Maybe you missed an important element of what she said. This isn't a test of right or wrong; it's about listening and making sure everyone is heard.

- **Be open and receptive for more input.** When she has agreed that you heard her correctly on that one comment, ask her, "Is there anything else you want to say?" Let her know that she has the floor until she's finished getting everything off her chest.

Staying on One Subject at a Time

By agreeing ahead of time to talk about only one topic and nothing else, couples can make significant progress on an issue. It might take several sessions to hear what the other has to say about a topic, just as it took some time for the feelings about the topic to develop. Be patient and keep talking. And give her this chapter to read, too.

I Am Woman, Hear Me Roar ... or Just Hear Me

Some fundamental differences between men and women can lead to conflict. By recognizing them, you can make a first step toward resolution.

Following are some of those differences:

- The most frequent complaint men have about women is this: Women are always trying to change them.
- The most frequent complaint women have about men is this: Men don't listen.
- Women want empathy, whereas men are more solution oriented.
- When a woman tries to change, improve, correct, or give a man advice, the man interprets it as being told he is incompetent or can't handle something alone.
- Men often feel responsible or blamed for women's problems.
- Men assume that the best way to be helpful to women is to offer advice or solutions to their problems; women often just want someone to sincerely listen to them.

 Groom Gambit

Be sure to keep in mind the fundamental differences between men and women when communicating about anything important, when expressing care and concern, and when solving conflicts.

- When women are upset, it's not the time to offer solutions; that is more appropriate at a future time when she's calmer.

- A man appreciates advice and criticism when it is requested. Men want to make improvements when they are approached as a solution to a problem rather than the problem itself.

- Men have great needs for status and independence (emphasis on separate and different); women have needs for intimacy and connection (close and same).

- Women need to experience caring, under-standing, respect, devotion, validation, and reassurance.

- Women are motivated when they feel special or cherished.

- Men need to experience trust, acceptance, appreciation, admiration, approval, and encouragement.

- Men are motivated when they feel needed. A man's deepest fear is that he is not good enough or not competent enough, although he might never express this.

These differences are not better or worse, just different. Of course, they are also generalizations; differences occur in all of us, and most of us carry some combination of "masculine" and "feminine" traits. To get along, however, you both must accept, expect, and respect these differences.

When you approach an unavoidable conflict, such as the earlier example of the basketball game, they key is compromise. For example, you might offer her a promise of something extra special the next day, reassure her that you respect her and your plans, and acknowledge that you hate to miss dinner with her but you also hate to pass up this opportunity. With any luck, she'll respect your need for independence, and trust that you'll make good on your next-day promise for something even better.

Inter-Family Communication

You can use the communication strategies presented here with anyone, not just with your fiancée. They can even be used with your in-laws, your new extended family.

Nuptial No-Nos

Though she may complain about her family until she's blue in the face, it's up to you to never, ever offer an unsolicited criticism of her relatives. This illogical rationale will become one of the fundamental tenets of your marriage.

Now that you're getting married, an important point to remember is that you're not only marrying your fiancée, you're also marrying her family. Her brother doesn't have to fill the role of your new best friend, but it'll save you a life's worth of headaches if you make some effort now to get along with him—and the rest of the family. If you already have a great relationship, good for you. You can stop reading now. If you don't, here are some surefire strategies for dealing with different types of in-laws.

The Over-Involved

You figure that they must be really bored because in addition to living their own lives, they're also trying to live yours. Either that or they're control freaks. This type of in-law is characterized by dropping in without warning, making plans for you without asking, assuming everything, and appeasing no one. Great diplomacy is necessary on your part, but you'll probably want to nip this overindulgence in the bud before it spirals madly out of control and you wake up to discover you're building an in-law apartment off your living room. Sometimes you just have to say no, even if you're trying like mad to please them and convey what a great guy you are.

The Under-Involved

These in-laws barely know your name, and you get the feeling it might take a few years before her dad actually has a conversation with you. Consider yourself lucky. Unless he genuinely doesn't like you, he's probably just distracted by work, gardening, golf—who really cares, as long as he's not distracted by *you*. If you're searching for a father figure, look elsewhere, but if you're happy to slide into a situation unnoticed, it's your lucky day.

The You're-Not-Quite-Good-Enough

When she's a true daddy's girl, daddy can be awfully hard to please. He might not verbalize it overtly, but his grunts and one-word answers signify to you his disapproval. If you believe it's totally unfounded—that he's basing his judgment on some superficialities beyond your control—take on the challenge of winning him over during the engagement period. That doesn't mean shameless brown-nosing; sometimes strong, silent actions are more effective. Show him how much you love his daughter in the little things you do, and make him confident that you will be a supportive husband and good provider. That's all daddy really cares about. (That and whether you're already sleeping with his daughter.)

The Tug-of-War Family

Mom hates Dad. Dad hates Mom. Your bride has been trying to achieve some balance in this circus act for years, and now it's your turn to jump into the ring. The engagement period in particular might be difficult because it's fraught with so many possibilities—and so many opportunities for disagreement. If disagreement is the cornerstone of your future parents-in-law's relationship, beware. Your best bet is to steer clear of the overt dysfunction and leave the challenging communications to your fiancée. She already knows the rules. But you can help her by providing an empathetic ear if things get too crazy, both during the engagement period and after you're married.

Groom Gambit

All it takes to solve a problem are two people willing to solve it, and two minds that are open enough to consider another option. Sometimes conflicts are even good for a relationship—their resolution can make a couple stronger.

Chapter 8

Pre-Wedding Events: What You Need to Know

In This Chapter

- The engagement party
- Bridal showers
- How to register for gifts, and why you might like it
- The rehearsal and dinner
- The politics of bachelor parties
- Bachelor party ideas

In the days from your engagement leading up to your wedding, you are the star. There will probably be more than one party that revolves around you—yes, you—in the time preceding your wedding, where you will be responsible for charming your bride's family, proving yourself to her dad, and graciously accepting blenders and other gifts you don't much care about. This is all part of the cult of weddings. Again, gender gaps are closing, so you might even be expected to attend a shower—unheard of in our parents' generation—*and* to help your bride register. We're here to tell you what to expect, how to make the best of it—and maybe even have fun in the process.

The Engagement Party

Not every couple has or is expected to have an engagement party, but just in case you do, here's the 411. Traditionally, the engagement party is thrown by either the parents of the groom or the parents of the bride. However, anyone can throw an engagement party, including a sibling, a favorite uncle, a co-worker, a friend—even the two of you as a couple. If you do decide to throw one for yourselves, be sure it's clear that you do not expect guests to bring gifts ("stick-'em-up" parties are tacky when self-arranged); you are inviting them for their good company and well wishes, not the booty they'll bring. If you are honored at an engagement party thrown by a friend or family, however, it's a common tradition for guests to bring gifts (unless, again, you specify otherwise). In the event you will be receiving gifts, be sure to register ahead of time. (See more on that subject later in this chapter.)

The engagement party was traditionally thrown to introduce the new couple to friends and relatives of the family. If you've been dating for a number of years, then you probably already know most of them; if so, consider yourself lucky. The party will be a lot easier if you're not meeting a large clan of unfamiliar people all at one time. If you *are* meeting a large number of unknowns, though, you must adopt the attitude you'd take to a job interview: Make sure you're properly showered, shaved, and pressed, and don't say anything too stupid. You will be judged for many years according to your behavior on this day. Make it work for you, not against you. Be gracious and charming, and you will reap great rewards.

◁ Nuptial No-Nos

When it comes to gifts (for the engagement, shower, and wedding), do not adopt a sense of entitlement. It's important to remember that gifts are optional for guests, *not* obligatory. While it's customary for guests to offer some token of celebration, do not allow the prospect of collecting gifts and money to overshadow what's truly meaningful about the wedding.

On engagement gifts—be sure to send out speedy thank-you notes acknowledging that you received and appreciated the gift-giver's generosity. For tips on writing memorable thank you notes, consult Appendix C.

Bridal Showers

Once strictly estrogen-only territory, showers, like weddings themselves, are evolving. Showers have traditionally been held to establish young couples emerging from their parents' homes with the household items they need to begin their new lives together. The bride would receive gifts like china, silver, linens, and kitchen appliances—everything necessary to establish a working household.

Today's showers are designed for much the same purpose, but occasionally feature a new twist: With brides and grooms getting married later, many engaged couples already have two households' full of things to merge. The last thing some couples need is a third coffeemaker or toaster oven. As a result, some couples' well-wishers throw showers centered on a theme, such as home improvement, where couples register at a store like Home Depot for items to fix up their house or apartment. Another "alternative" theme is a honeymoon shower, at which guests contribute to your honeymoon, which you've registered for through a travel agent. Even sports or hobbies can function as a theme; avid skiers, for instance, would receive ski equipment, ski passes, or ski wear. Basically, the options are endless, although you probably will still, somewhere down the line, receive another toaster.

Another trend that you may or may not appreciate is the emergence of co-ed showers (also known as Jack-and-Jill showers). Yes, you may be expected to attend this gathering, formerly only the province of women, where you must eat crudités, drink punch and wine, and open gift after gift in front of a large group of people intent on your happy reactions to their particular offering. Sound like fun? Just keep in mind that you're probably having more fun than your father, who's also forced to be there; at least you get something to take home at the end of the night.

 Groom Gambit _____

> If you are given a co-ed shower, you will be expected to join your future bride in opening gifts. Be sure to be gracious, thanking each gift-giver individually by name and, if possible, making a personal comment about the gift, such as, "This wok will be terrific when I cook my wife dinner after a long day." In other words, it's a great suck-up opportunity.

Actually, if approached with the right mindset, co-ed showers can be a lot of fun; your friends are there, her friends are there, and your family rounds out the group. These showers can turn into full-scale parties similar to an engagement party, with good food and spirits paving the way for a fun evening.

Collecting the Loot

As mentioned earlier in this chapter, you will be receiving a great number of gifts during your engagement … and for up to a year after your wedding. This is a perk of weddings that you may have forgotten. If your idea of an exciting gift is not a food processor, however, do not despair. "Household" items can also include choice goodies like stereos, espresso makers, DVD players … do I have your interest yet? In other words, it's up to you and your bride what kind of loot you'll *register* for.

Wedding Words

Registering is the process of creating a "wish list" of household items you'd like to receive as wedding and shower gifts, through a department or specialty store or both. Registering makes guests' choices of gifts easy and guarantees that you'll receive the items you need in the right quantities.

If you think that registering for your wedding is akin to asking people for gifts, you're right. However, this is the one time that formal etiquette allows—even promotes—such overt greediness. In reality, registering for gifts actually saves your guests much time and anxiety over choosing a gift; it provides an organized way for couples to receive the items they really need, without duplication. Your guests are most likely going to give you a gift anyway; why not make it something that you actually need and that your guests will be confident you'll appreciate?

There are a few rules to registering:

Rule #1. First, you can register in more than one place; in fact, that's probably the preferable way to do things if you're having a medium- to large-sized wedding. With multiple registrations, your guests will have a choice about where they can purchase your gift, which makes it more convenient. You can register at stores ranging from Tiffany to Target, with department stores and specialty stores such as Pier One and Pottery Barn in between. Shop around a bit before you decide where you definitely want to register.

Rule #2. Be sure to register for gifts in different price ranges. Not all your guests want to buy you a $100 china place setting for a shower gift, and there are only a handful of guests—okay, probably none—who'll shell out enough to afford that plasma TV you've been eyeing. Make sure you have enough lower-priced items to balance your list, even if guests feel the need to buy you three smaller items.

Nuptial No-Nos

Don't register for more than your guest list can handle; consult a sales associate to determine the proper number of items and price ranges to choose from. You don't want to end up with half the number of place settings, silver, or glassware that you've registered for, unless you want to cough up a generous chunk of cash later to finish off your collections.

Rule #3. Timing is everything. If you're having an engagement that lasts longer than a year, a good rule of thumb is to wait at least six months before registering (unless you're having a major party such as a shower or engagement party before that). The reason you should wait is that store inventory changes, and you don't want to start a set of crystal glasses or china that the store will discontinue carrying in eight months.

But don't wait too long; as mentioned previously, you want to register before you have any major parties so that guests have more options, and so you can begin receiving gifts based on exactly what you want and need.

Rule #4. You don't have to register for the traditional china, crystal, and linens that your parents registered for. Couples are choosing all sorts of creative options, such as registries online or at nontraditional stores, for more practical items that

they really need and may not have already. For
example, if you already have two sets of dishes,
glassware, and silverware, why not register for a
barbecue grill or lawnmower—two items you'll
inevitably need or want down the line? Or, you can
register for furniture: One guest doesn't have to
purchase the whole thing. Rather, multiple guests
can contribute to a registry item that adds up to
the total price. Check with your favorite stores to
learn their specific policies and advice regarding
nontraditional registering. Remember, it doesn't
hurt to ask any store to set up a registry for you,
even if they don't regularly offer this service. After
all, you're bringing them some serious business in
exchange for the minimal effort it will take to set
up your registry.

Rule #5. Formal etiquette dictates that it is proper
to include registry information in the shower invitation, but not in the wedding invitation. (Some
people aren't comfortable with either option.) Rely
on friends and relatives to spread the word about
where you're registered for wedding gifts.

Many stores will offer you a one-year discount
following your wedding to purchase any remaining
items on your registry, so you can complete un-
finished sets of dishes, glasses, appliances, and
cookware that you've received. Many stores will
keep your information on hand for at least a year
so that procrastinating guests can still consult it up
to the etiquette-inspired year's deadline they have
to buy you a wedding gift.

The following are the traditional lists of items couples use as a gift registry guide. Remember, it's fine to stray off the list, but don't forget that the china that seems overly expensive and impractical now will become a necessary evil when you start entertaining friends, family, and business associates in the not-so-distant future.

Tableware (8 to 12 five-piece formal place settings):

- Dinner plate
- Salad/dessert plate
- Bread-and-butter plate
- Cup
- Saucer

You might also want to order a casual or transitional pattern to be dressed up or down in addition to your formal china.

Additional tableware pieces:

- Platter
- Vegetable bowls
- Gravy boat
- Sugar bowl and creamer
- Salt and pepper shakers

Glassware (same quantity as dinnerware):

- Goblets
- Iced-beverage glasses

- All-purpose wine glasses
- Champagne flutes
- Double old-fashioned glasses

Flatware (same quantity as dinnerware):

- Dinner fork
- Dinner knife
- Soup spoon
- Salad/dessert fork
- Tea/dessert spoon

You can choose from sterling silver, silver plate, or stainless steel (with prices that reflect each option). You might want to register for two sets—formal and casual.

Additional pieces of flatware:

- Hostess set
- Salad serving set
- Extra teaspoons
- Extra salad forks

Cookware (register for boxed sets or individual pieces):

- 10" frying pan or skillet
- 8-quart stockpot
- Grill or griddle
- 2-quart and 3-quart saucepans
- Roasting pan

If you fancy yourself somewhat of a gourmet, you'll probably want to register for high-quality, commercial-grade pots and pans. Copper pans are best for equal heat distribution—plus they look great.

Linens: Bedroom

- 3 sets of sheets
- 3 sets of pillowcases
- Comforter and duvet
- Bed skirt
- Pillows
- Blankets

Linens: Bathroom

- 2 sets of hand towels per bathroom
- 2 sets of face towels per bathroom
- 2 sets of bath towels per bathroom
- Shower curtains
- Bath mats
- Guest towels

Linens: Kitchen

- 2 to 4 sets of table linens. Consider choosing one formal set in damask, lace, or linen
- Place mats and napkins

Choose colors, patterns, and fabrics that will mix and match. Unless you're particularly interested, you may want to let your bride coordinate colors for linens. If you're not sure about a color scheme for your house yet, choose neutral colors.

Kitchenware:

- Blender
- Coffeemaker
- Slow cooker
- Electric can opener
- Food processor
- Hand mixer
- Toaster or toaster oven
- Microwave
- Bread maker

Cutlery:

- 8" chef's knife
- Bread knife
- Paring knife
- Utility knife
- Sharpening steel
- Pair of kitchen shears
- Knife block to hold them all
- 8 to 12 steak knives

Additional items:

- Garlic press
- Mixing spoons
- Spatulas

- Cheese grater
- Measuring cups and spoons
- Vegetable peeler

Here are some ideas beyond the basics:

- Electronics, including a fax machine, an alarm clock, or a CD or DVD player
- Giftware, including vases, picture frames, and candlesticks
- Necessities for the home, including an iron, ironing board, smoke alarm, or shower massage

These recommendations should have you covered for the very basics. For more guidance, make an appointment with your favorite department or specialty store, where a sales associate will assist you in coordinating patterns and tailoring your list to the number of guests. Or, begin searching online for registries with styles you like.

Rehearsal Dinner

Another of the pre-wedding events—the rehearsal dinner—is typically held one to two days before the wedding. The rehearsal dinner usually follows the ceremony rehearsal, where the bride, groom, bridesmaids, groomsmen, and other honored participants are coached on the proceedings of the ceremony so they won't screw up too badly during the main event. The groom's family traditionally throws the dinner that follows, but as with the wedding expenses, the cost can be split according to your individual situation.

The dinner can be anything from a formal sit-down meal to a more casual, backyard-type affair, depending on your preferences and what your parents have in mind. If you'd like, this is the one area where you can really get involved, in light of the fact that your parents are probably planning it (or perhaps you're doing it yourself). In any event, the rehearsal dinner is a big part of the wedding festivities and can often be just as much fun—if not more fun—than the wedding day, if only because it's a bit more intimate.

Groom Gambit

It is traditional to give your groomsmen a special gift for taking part in your wedding. (See specific gift ideas in Appendix B.) The rehearsal dinner is the most popular time to present groomsmen with their gifts.

The guest list at the rehearsal dinner should include the bride and groom, your parents, your siblings and their spouses or guests, your grand-parents, the wedding party and ceremony partici-pants and their spouses or guests, and optionally, any out-of-town guests. It's also nice to invite the clergyperson performing your ceremony, especially if he or she is a friend of the family.

It is customary for the bride and groom to say a few words at the rehearsal dinner, thanking their parents and guests for their love and support. Toasts/speeches may precede or follow dinner. Your father might also want to say a few words, as he is this evening's host. The floor is then open to anyone who wants to make a toast, including the best man, maid of honor, or other guests who wish to honor the bride and groom.

Be careful not to stay out too late—or drink too much—if your rehearsal dinner is the night before the wedding. It'll probably be tempting; you'll be excited and maybe a little nervous, and all your friends and close family will want to celebrate with you, too. Just keep in mind that the next day is one of the most important in your life. You want to be well rested and clear headed—not to mention look good for the photos and video you'll be stuck with forever.

The Bachelor Party (a.k.a. How Much Do You Love Your Bride?)

Chances are, you've already been to a few bachelor parties and are already well aware of the chain of events—liquor, gambling, and the requisite dancing girls, not necessarily in that order. The object of this night is, ultimately, to abuse such vices in pursuit of some unnamed or unidentified goal, resulting in behavior you wouldn't be proud of if your mother found out.

For whatever reason, men revel in this sort of excess. Pre-marriage, it is the ultimate exercise in independence, proving once and for all that a man can still do what a man wants to do. In this spirit, you might end up offending your bride; tread carefully during this sensitive time right before the wedding. Between the Internet, TV, and movies, women today are fully aware of what can happen at these parties, so if you must take part in activities of which she would not approve, keep it as tame and respectful as possible. One exercise to help put it all in perspective is imagining your bride out with her girlfriends, picking up some Johnny Depp look-a-like with whom she ends up entangled before coming home to you. Probably not on your top-ten list of favorite images.

Aside from their bad rap among the female population, there are plenty of worthwhile activities surrounding the bachelor party, including spending quality time with a large group of friends (or a small group, depending on your preference). Anything where her father would be comfortable is known as a "gentleman's bachelor party"; that is, you're doing nothing to make him feel he should start cleaning his gun collection anytime soon.

Word to the wise: If you can't stand the heat, get out of the kitchen. Post-bachelor party residue can get ugly, so the key is being honest and respectful. The rest is up to you.

Bachelor-Party Ideas

A bachelor party is simply meant to be a celebration prior to one's wedding. In that vein, there are countless activities you can plan, ranging from an evening barhopping to a weekend excursion. The following are some ideas to consider for your own bachelor party; drop (obvious and clear) hints to your best man so that he can plan the party you want.

House Party

Probably the simplest of the bachelor party choices, a house party can be kicked up a notch if the details are well attended to. Instead of the old beer-and-stale-chips party, splurge on single-malt scotches, good cigars, and catered food. If it's summertime, torch the backyard fire pit and regale each other with old stories by firelight. Stay up 'til the sun rises.

Renting a Bar or Restaurant

One popular bachelor party tradition is renting out (part or all) of a bar or restaurant for a few hours of drinking, gambling, and socializing. Your best man and groomsmen will spread the word by sending or passing out invitations with the requisite information about time, date, and place. Typically, a donation is requested in a specific dollar amount to help cover the costs of an open bar and some munchies, with any leftover funds earmarked as a "gift for the bride." In other words, it's a little bribe for your honey to ease up on you the morning after.

To maximize the fun, be sure your activities are organized. If you'd like to have tables for gambling, for instance, assign a groomsman the task of organizing some gaming tables, including buying plenty of decks of cards, poker chips, and any other desired equipment (a roulette wheel, a craps table, etc.). If you want to incorporate dealer-oriented games, like blackjack or roulette, assign another friend or groomsman to act as dealer.

You may also wish to organize raffles to give partygoers the chance to win cash or prizes. For prizes, ask friends and family for donations, or ask friendly bar-owners or beer distributors if they have anything they wouldn't mind unloading. Sell an "arm's-length" of raffle tickets for a few bucks, and then pull tickets later on for the winners. For a "50–50 split" raffle, partygoers have the chance to receive a cash prize. The 50–50 split works by giving half the total take to whomever's holding the winning ticket, and the other half to the bride for honeymoon expenses (further bribery). Just be sure not to lose all that cash to some stripper's G-string before the night's over.

Destination Bachelor Party

Growing increasingly popular is the destination bachelor party, whereby you and your friends party for an entire weekend (or longer, if you can get away with it) somewhere other than your hometown. These destinations can range from the wild, such as New Orleans or Las Vegas, to the comparatively tame, such as a golf resort. The advantages of the destination bachelor party are the ability to get away from it all, the time factor (two or three days are more fun than one), and activities or attractions that may not be available locally. The disadvantages are cost and effort, both of which will end up demanding more than a party planned closer to home. You also run the risk of alienating potential partygoers due to the built-in financial or logistical challenges of a weekend away. If this is the case, you may wish to also have a party close to home.

To plan a destination bachelor party, talk to your best man about details. Choose a location, and then float a few possible dates to your friends and groomsmen, so that you can choose the best weekend to go. If you have enough partygoers, you may even be eligible for a group rate on airlines or at a hotel/resort—be sure to look into these details before booking your trip.

Activity-Based Bachelor Party

Pick your favorite activity. Then force all your friends to enjoy it, too. Chances are, you won't have to force them too much if your ideal activity is something like golf, boating, or a night of Texas Hold 'Em. Organizing your party around a hobby or sport can be a great way to spend quality time with friends and family, especially if you haven't all gotten together in a while. The following are some more ideas for an activity-based get-together:

- Rent a large fishing boat and go on a day-long excursion.

- Mountain bike a promising new trail.
- Ski or snowboard. Enjoy chalet cocktails afterward.
- Go hunting. (Very manly)
- Waterski or wakeboard.
- Snorkel or scuba-dive (i.e., "take the plunge").
- Skydive.
- Go to a sporting event—football, basketball, baseball, or hockey game.
- Organize a giant baseball, touch football, or roller-hockey game.
- Go to the racetrack or a casino (horses, jai alai, etc.).
- Rent a lakeside house or cabin in the woods.
- Enjoy a really decadent steakhouse.

Bachelor Party Aftermath

If you've had a particularly wild night of debauchery (and your fiancée was apprehensive about the party in the first place), a little damage control the following day can never hurt. Set her mind at ease by calling her in the morning to let her know you're still alive, that you love her, that you missed her the night before (okay, so stretch the truth a little), and that you can't wait to be her husband.

Later in the day bring her flowers or a little gift, take her out to a nice dinner, or stay in for a night of cozy cuddling and movie rentals. In other words, make up for any craziness from the night before by being extra attentive, charming, and groomlike. It'll be worth the extra effort—promise.

Chapter 9

Finally the Good Stuff: Honeymoon Planning

In This Chapter

- Types of honeymoons
- The honeymoon planner
- Popular honeymoon destinations
- Preparing and packing

For most men, planning a honeymoon invokes one of two reactions—great anticipation or serious dread. After all, this might be the first real trip you need to plan—somewhat different from the usual wake up, throw some stuff in a duffel bag, gas up the car, and hope it gets you to your buddy's place in New York City/San Francisco/Chicago without breaking down first. If you haven't been on an extended trip with your fiancée yet, here is one great truth you will soon learn: Traveling with women is very different from traveling by yourself, or with your guy friends. Generally speaking, women are more organized. Women are more careful with their planning. Most women plan what they'll need to pack weeks in advance so that they can go shopping.

If you follow traditional etiquette, you, as the groom, are charged with planning this Cadillac of all trips. With an endless number of destinations and potential activities, it's a heady responsibility. You will need a structured plan to ensure that you and your bride end up with a room to sleep in and some things to do during the day—or at the very least, gas in your car.

Types of Honeymoons

So there's a world of destination possibilities and you've barely been across state lines. A honeymoon is your one great excuse to be extravagant—to go somewhere you've never gone before, spend more cash on a hotel than you could ever otherwise justify, and do something totally impractical. With all these options, where's a guy to start? The following checklist will help you narrow down the unlimited options you face, so you can start thinking seriously about where you're going to end up.

Check the top three most interesting or important activities for you and your bride on your honeymoon:

- Relaxing on a beach
- Casino gambling
- Golfing

- Playing water sports
- Playing tennis
- Skiing
- Trying adventure sports (whitewater rafting, mountain climbing, and so on)
- Seeing a new city
- Touring a number of cities
- Touring museums
- Touring art galleries
- Touring historical sites
- Touring natural wonders (volcanoes, waterfalls, and so on)
- Shopping
- Fine dining
- Exploring a new culture
- Backpacking
- Experiencing great nightlife
- Getting away from it all
- Pampering from a spa
- Attending special events (Olympics, bullfighting, Mardi Gras, Tour de France, and so on)

Once you've chosen your top three interests, it becomes much easier to narrow down your options. For instance, if you've chosen gambling, beaches, and great nightlife, there's Aruba or Monte Carlo. If you've chosen fine dining, shopping, and muse-ums, any cosmopolitan city in the world will do, from Paris to Sydney to Rio to New York. Got the idea? Once you have an idea of the type of vacation you want, you'll be able to pick and choose your destination based on budgetary, timing, and travel considerations.

Your next step is to consult a travel agent, who will have a lot of ideas about where your interests can be found. Ask around for references to a good travel agent. If you are a do-it-yourselfer, begin researching online, where you can find great deals, or look in the travel section of your local bookstore. See Appendix A for some starting points.

 **Groom Gambit** _____

> Your options are unlimited when it comes to the types of activities for your honeymoon. Provided that your bride is game, you can make a beach getaway, sightsee in Europe, join an African safari, or hike Antarctica. Your honeymoon is one vacation where you'll feel justified being a little extravagant.

Honeymoon Planner

It's always easier to plan with a timeline. The following lists will take you from six months before your vacation to the day before you leave, so that you won't forget any important honeymoon details:

At least six months in advance …

- Investigate possible destinations. Use the preceding checklist to narrow down your choices, and then consult with a travel agent, friends and family, and the Internet for options and referrals.

- Reserve airline tickets and get a confirmation number.

- Reserve hotels and specify the type of room (smoking, beachfront, and so on).

- Reserve a rental car and get a confirmation number.

- Consider purchasing travel insurance to protect your investment from unforeseen complications.

- Sign up for foreign language classes or buy tapes if you're going abroad.

Three months in advance …

- Obtain passports.
- Finalize all reservations.

Two months ahead …

- Make a shopping list of items you'll need for the trip (such as film, batteries, and an electrical adapter if traveling abroad).

- Get the proper vaccinations.

One month ahead ...

- Confirm all reservations.
- Order special meals from the airlines.
- Book tours, tee times, theater tickets, massages, dinners, and other activities that require reservations through your travel agent, tour operator, or hotel concierge. (Note that many resorts will claim you need to book activities ahead of time, but often you don't. Keep some free time in your schedule to account for downtime or spontaneity.
- Make arrangements for dog- or cat-sitting, plant watering, or house-sitting.
- Get any prescriptions or medications you can't do without.

Two weeks ahead ...

- Pick up tickets, boarding passes, transfers, and vouchers from the travel agent.
- Buy travelers' checks, and copy the numbers of checks onto a separate sheet of paper in case they're lost or stolen.

One week ahead ...

- Arrange to have mail held at the post office or ask someone to pick it up periodically at your home.

- Stop newspaper delivery; a pile of newspapers on your doorstep is a thief's welcome mat.
- Ask the stores where you've registered to temporarily stop deliveries, or arrange for someone to pick up gift deliveries.
- Begin packing.
- Organize addresses to write thank-you notes on the plane (you'll be happy to get it over with!).

Three days ahead ...

- Reconfirm overseas flights.
- Buy books or magazines for the plane and poolside.
- Arrange transportation to and from the airport.
- Leave your itinerary and phone numbers with a relative in case of emergency.
- Check the weather reports for your destination.

One day ahead ...

- Reconfirm domestic flights.
- Get your house ready for departure: Take out the garbage, clean out the fridge, set timers, and so on.

>◁✑ **Nuptial No-Nos**
>
> Don't forget to pay the bills that will be
> due while you're away, especially if
> you're going on an extended honey-
> moon. Also, check your credit-card
> balances before you leave to be sure
> that there's plenty of room for honeymoon
> indulgences—or emergencies.

Popular Honeymoon Destinations

Back in the day, Niagara Falls was the king of honeymoon destinations, with thousands of honeymooners and celebrities visiting every year. The
Falls are still there, but the romance has been
replaced by wax museums, The Hard Rock café,
Planet Hollywood, and a great big casino. A sign of
the times, perhaps ....

In our mobile society, today's honeymooners are
more likely to travel outside the United States,
from the Caribbean to Europe to the South
Pacific. Smart resorts now market themselves to
extravagance-prone honeymooners, and cater to
couples once they arrive. The following sections,
while by no means a comprehensive list, describe
some of today's hot honeymoon destinations.

The Caribbean

With a seemingly endless list of islands to choose
from, the Caribbean has a lot to offer for those

seeking a beach honeymoon with any number of variations, such as golf, water sports, gambling, sightseeing, shopping, and nightlife. There seems to be an island for every interest, depending on your priorities. For secluded beaches, gorgeous gardens, and a slightly formal atmosphere, visit Bermuda. St. Lucia offers the natural beauty of mountains, rain forests, and a more rustic feel, with West Indian culture. Aruba is known for its spectacular blue water, great beaches, and glittering casinos. Jamaica, one of the largest islands, has a host of options, including many *all-inclusive resorts*.

Wedding Words

An **all-inclusive resort** offers a pay-one-price package deal that includes such amenities as airfare, accommodations, meals, drinks, and sports and activities. Be sure to verify the details before booking, so that you know exactly what's included. The beauty of all-inclusives is that there are no hidden costs; you don't have to think about money once you're there, even for tipping. Popular resorts include Sandals, Super Clubs, Breezes, Couples, and Club Med. Individual resorts also offer all-inclusive deals. Be sure to do your research—the quality of resorts, food, and even drinks can vary tremendously.

Hawaii

Hawaii is arguably the most popular honeymoon destination for American newlyweds. Travel agents credit the romantic atmosphere, laid-back environment, beautiful natural surroundings, endless stretches of beaches, and island history to Hawaii's never-ending draw of tourists. And you don't even need a passport to get there.

Hawaii's attractions are split among the six islands, which include Maui, Kauai, The Big Island, Oahu, Lanai, and Molokai. Maui is the most popular honeymoon spot, with its great beaches, diving, and activities such as biking, water sports, and helicopter rides. There are some beautiful Maui resorts both near the center of the action and farther away from it; you can take your pick.

Kauai's lush natural beauty is marked by gorgeous waterfalls, cliffs, and sea caves. The Big Island is great for couples interested in sightseeing, golfing, and volcano hiking. For couples seeking a lot of activity, Oahu is home to Waikiki Beach, which is swarming with restaurants, nightlife, and surfers from around the world. There are plenty of other activities as well, including kayaking, hiking, and traditional games and crafts.

For those seeking more seclusion, Hawaii's islands of Lanai or Molokai are true getaways. They are both secluded and dedicated to preserving their natural resources. Lanai is mostly rugged terrain, with only two ultra-upscale hotels.

👍 **Groom Gambit** _____

> Don't miss one of Hawaii's traditional luaus. A luau, if you'll recall, is a beach party like the one attended by the Brady family at the end of their big Hawaiian trip (after Greg, Peter, and Bobby got rid of the cursed Tiki, of course). Luaus are filled with great food—usually a pig roast—music, and dancing—particularly that of a belly nature.(It's the one time you can get away with checking out other women on your honeymoon.)

Europe

There are so many worthwhile destinations in Europe that it's difficult to go into detail on any of them. But here goes: If you're seeking history and culture, including museums, galleries, and architecture, why not try London, Paris, Madrid, Berlin, Amsterdam, Athens, Rome, or Venice? Or, to narrow your options, why not travel to your ancestors' homelands? If you're Italian and she's Irish, travel to both countries to learn about your background *and* have an unforgettable honeymoon. If you'd like to experience the greatest number of cities in the least amount of time, buy Eurail passes and travel from country to country. If you decide to do a bit of traveling, be sure to establish an itinerary ahead of time so that you get the accommodations that you desire in each city.

There's nothing worse than scrounging around for vacancies when you're dead tired and you just want to relax, especially in a foreign country.

If you're seeking Europe by seaside, you've still got a lot of options, such as the French Riviera and Monaco; Estoril, Portugal; Italy's Amalfi coast; and Barcelona, Spain. These destinations also offer big-city attractions such as fine restaurants and sightseeing.

French Polynesia

The islands of Tahiti and Bora Bora in the South Pacific are a honeymooner's dream. Although it'll take you some time to get there (you're flying literally halfway around the world), tourists say it's worth the trip. You might wish to extend your honeymoon by a few days if you travel this far, however, to get over jet lag and to have enough time to truly decompress.

The islands are exotic and romantic, and offer fantastic diving and gorgeous beaches. Their spectacular scenery includes mountains, tropical rainforests, and quaint South Seas ports. Affordable package deals are available, especially if you choose to island hop; check with a travel agent for the best deals.

The Good Old U.S. of A.

In today's often-unstable international environment, many honeymooners are rediscovering the comfort and appeal of the mainland United States. Fortunately, there are plenty of great destinations for honeymooners, including such diverse options as South Beach in Miami, an art-deco cosmopolitan beach community infused with nonstop nightlife and hordes of beautiful people. Or why not drive the Pacific Coast Highway and splurge on fabulous hotels along the way in Malibu, Big Sur, and Beverly Hills? Or you could try Savannah or Charleston, cities rich with history and old southern charm. And, of course, there's always New York City, with its endless attractions and world-renowned restaurants, hotels, and shopping—a city that's more tourist friendly and financially desirable than ever for vacationers.

Here are a few more options to consider: Lake Tahoe, straddling the borders of Nevada and California; the Poconos in Pennsylvania; Colorado for adventure sports and skiing; Arizona for premier golf; Hilton Head Island for golf and tennis; New Orleans for sightseeing, culture, and revelry; or Las Vegas for gambling, warm weather, and great deals on hotels and restaurants. Check with friends, relatives, and a travel agent for additional ideas.

Cruises

Cruises are a great way to experience many ports of call with minimal worry about travel or finances. Their all-inclusive nature appeals to honeymooners who want to pay up-front for a stress-free vacation.

Cruises are well-regarded for their top-of-the-line unlimited menus—many cruises even offer 24-hour dining—and diverse entertainment, all included in one price. You can find great deals on cruises with two-for-one options and free room upgrades, if you keep your eyes open. Cruises are popular among honeymooners, so chances are, you'll meet other couples in the same boat (no pun intended). Cruises are also known to pamper guests, especially honeymooners.

The most popular cruises for Americans tend to be those among the Caribbean islands, Mexico, and the Bahamas. But cruises are also available in more exotic destinations such as Alaska, the Greek Islands, Turkey, and the South Pacific. Some cruises stop at private islands for water sports and other activities.

Consult with a travel agent before booking a cruise, or do some homework yourself on the Internet. All cruises are not created equal, so be sure to get referrals from people you trust before booking. Some of the more popular and reputable cruise lines include Royal Caribbean, Carnival, Princess Cruises, Celebrity Cruises, and Holland America. The newer ships are usually nicer, and some are more inherently upscale than others. Be sure to check with your travel agent for options.

If you've got an unlimited budget, you can have a truly unforgettable cruise. Luxury ships offer personalized service and amenities to match their price tags. Upscale cabins offer such extras as private balconies, private Jacuzzis, or king-sized beds. Romantic destinations such as Europe, the South Pacific, and the Orient can make a mediocre cruise shine. The motto of cruises? If you want it, it's out there.

Groom Gambit

To get the biggest bang for your cruise buck, follow a few strategies. Book early to get the best deal; get your specific room request guaranteed (such as an out-side cabin with balcony); and be flexible about your vacation priorities. If you want the best room, you might have to forgo booking on the newest ship, for instance.

The drawback of cruises is that your options are somewhat limited by the ever-moving nature of the cruise; you might be able to spend only a few hours in ports where you'd like to stay longer. You are also assigned a table for dinner for the duration of the cruise—so if you get stuck with irritating people, you're in for some long, potentially annoying meals.

How to Pack

So you've chosen your destination, you're following your planning timeline to a T, and now it's time to pack. Unless you've gone to military school, chances are you're a sloppy packer. Most men are; it's a metaphor for why to get married, really. In the event that your wife-to-be is not packing for you, here are some sure-fire tips that you'll use for your honeymoon and beyond:

- Pack in advance. Waiting until the last minute only causes stress when you realize that many of your clothing favorites are rumpled, stained, or missing.

- Check the weather predictions for your destination a day in advance, in case any unexpected climate changes are blowing through the area.

- Bring necessities from home, such as sunscreen, medications, and especially prescriptions. You might not be able to get the types you need—or you'll pay a premium for them.

- Pack toiletries that could leak in a plastic bag. There's nothing worse than arriving at your destination with a bag full of clothing covered in hair gel or shampoo.

- Carry valuables or one-of-a-kind items such as glasses or jewelry in your carry-on bag. You just never know when a bag could end up in airline limbo.

- Make sure you label all luggage.

- Pack enough, but pack lightly. You'll want some room left for honeymoon souvenirs!

Chapter **10**

Looking Your Best: Grooming for Guys

In This Chapter

- Choosing the right formalwear
- Shave and a haircut …
- Choosing a wedding ring

The details are planned and the countdown has begun. You're either relieved or starting to sweat more by the day. No matter how little or how much you've already been involved in this wedding-planning process, a few additional considerations will require a bit of thought on your part—unless you want to set the ultimate precedent for this union, forfeiting independent thought for life. You'll definitely want input into such decisions as your formalwear and your wedding ring; after all, what you're wearing is the ultimate reflection of your personality and style. And you might want to put a little extra effort into your usual five-minute daily grooming routine so that you can look your best—at least for this one day. This chapter is meant to guide you in these murky decision-making waters—so that you don't look all washed up.

Puttin' on the Ritz

Even if your wedding is casual, you should put some serious thought into what you choose to wear on your wedding day. Here are a few immediate tips:

- Don't wear something you even remotely think you'll cringe at seeing in 20 years.

- Don't choose something just because it's outrageous, even if your typical modus operandi is less than conservative. Your wedding day is a serious event, and your clothing should reflect that gravity.

- Choose something classic that fits well and reflects your taste. If your bride is steering you to wear something you just won't feel comfortable in (such as a loud cummerbund or top hat and tails), then change direction and choose what you want. This is your wedding day, too, don't forget.

On your wedding day, you want to make a statement. Your statement, mind you, should speak volumes in its style and subtlety. Your wedding, I regret to inform you, is not the ideal place to don your Disney characters bow tie and vest. Nor is it the time to go on the cheap. If you're renting, as the majority of men do, spend a little extra on the style, colors, and fabrics that best suit you. Or take this opportunity to finally purchase a tuxedo, especially if you have a more active formal social calendar. To women, a well-made, tailored-to-fit tuxedo is akin to a thong bathing suit from a man's perspective: It turns heads. Just look at James Bond's tuxedoed charm.

Whether you're renting or buying, you have many styles to choose from. Here's a crash course in formalwear to get the ball rolling.

Groom Gambit

Some men eschew the formal tuxedo altogether. One groom chose a well-cut suit for his wedding and subsidized matching suits for his groomsmen. Three years later, former groomsmen are still being spotted around town in their well-worn wedding suits—making the money that would have gone toward a one-time tux rental a great investment.

Jacket Styles

It's helpful to start with a working knowledge of jacket styles, so you can choose the one that best "suits" you:

- **Single-breasted.** This jacket has one row of buttons down the front. Single-breasted jackets come with one-, two-, three-, and four-button styles, so choose the style that you like best. Generally, the more buttons you choose, the taller and narrower you should be for it to flatter. Barrel-chested or stout men might look a bit like stuffed sausages in higher-buttoned jackets.

- **Double-breasted.** David Letterman's signature jacket. Traditionally, they're a bit boxy, but in recent years, shaped double-breasted jackets have become the trend. Any body type can look good in this style—and it can be an especially good one to choose if you want to hide a few extra pounds.

- **Tails.** Highly formal, this jacket is characterized by its short-in-front, long-in-back design—kinda like your high-school mullet. Short, stout men might want to steer clear of this style, which can make them look penguin-like.

- **Cutaway** (a.k.a. a morning coat). Looking good on just about any frame, this jacket tapers from the waistline button to one broad tail in the back, with a vent. Very Kennedy. Very silver screen.

- **Dinner jacket.** Single- or double-breasted jacket in white, ivory, or novelty fabrics worn with black, satin-striped trousers.

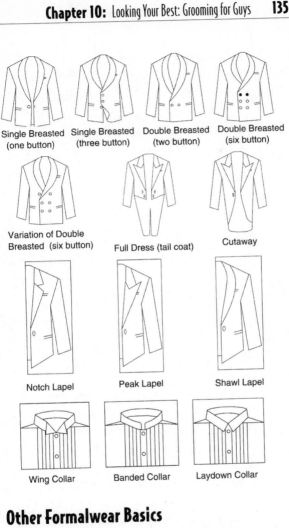

Single Breasted (one button)   Single Breasted (three button)   Double Breasted (two button)   Double Breasted (six button)

Variation of Double Breasted (six button)   Full Dress (tail coat)   Cutaway

Notch Lapel   Peak Lapel   Shawl Lapel

Wing Collar   Banded Collar   Laydown Collar

Other Formalwear Basics

The jacket style you choose helps dictate your other formalwear options, including vests, trousers, and neckwear. For instance, if you choose a cutaway coat, you should choose a low vest and ascot for the classic look that complements this jacket. But if you choose a single- or double-breasted jacket, your options are more flexible:

- **High vest.** Vests are where you can really express your individuality. High vests look best on taller, narrower men. If you're very broad chested, choose a vest that's muted, not too bright.

Groom Gambit

Have each of your attendants get his formalwear properly fitted ahead of time in case there are any problems. The sooner any mishaps are detected, the more time you'll have to solve the problem.

- **Low vest.** Generally, these look good on all men, except in the cases where they can look like belly slings. Large beer bellies should steer clear.

- **Bow tie.** You wore a clip-on to the prom. This time, choose one you have to tie yourself.

- **Four-in-hand tie.** Very now. This knotted tie hangs vertically, like a business-suit tie. It should be worn with a spread collar (business-shirt collar).

- **Ascot.** Very society. Broad neck scarf looped under the chin, fastened with a tie tack or stickpin, and worn with a wing collar.

- **Wing collar.** Collar with downward points; looks great with an ascot or bow tie.

- **Laydown collar.** Similar to a business-shirt collar.

- **Mandarin or banded collar.** Think priest's collar crossed with Euro style. No tie is worn. Avoid this if you've got a thick, short, or heavy neck.

Unless you regularly read *GQ* and know the definition of "couture," you may also want your bride's input as to the most flattering and appropriate style for your wedding.

Formalwear Sizing

An ill-fitting tuxedo is one of the sadder things in life. The implication is that you care enough to don some serious formalwear but that you have poor follow-through. Or worse, that you've settled for a cheap rental. Maybe some other time you can get away with it. But on your wedding day, honor the occasion with a tux that fits well. Here are a few tips to ensure that you're in good shape:

- Choose a store that has a tailor on the premises. If pant legs don't fit, they can be hemmed or let out in 10 minutes. If there's no tailor on site, ask the store in advance whether it has an affiliation with a tailor who'll do last-minute alterations.

- If you're renting, pick up your tux as early as possible—preferably a day or two in advance. That way, the store will have more time to fix any problems.

- Shirts should hug the neck and be neither too loose nor too tight.

- Pants should just touch the top of shoes.

- Waistbands are often adjustable; check for side buckles.

- Jacket should fit snugly but comfortably around shoulders, with some room at the waist, and no arm bulges.

- Collar should hug the neck, and lapels shouldn't buckle.

- Jacket sleeves should end at the wrist bone.

Nuptial No-Nos

Don't forget to return any rented formalwear after your wedding; you can end up being charged by the day for late returns. If you are leaving for your honeymoon immediately following the wedding, appoint a (trusted) groomsman—or ask your father—to return yours when he returns his own.

Beyond Threads

Of course, there's more to looking good than your monkey suit. As your bride can attest from years of

experience, it takes a certain regimen for your
hair and skin to look healthy and vibrant, for your
body to be in top shape, and for your hands and
nails to be clean and neat. And while this all may
be too much effort for the off-season (i.e., after the
wedding), looking your best for your important day
will be well worth the extra work.

A Proper Shave

A good shave that prevents razor burn or rash isn't
rocket science, but it does take a little effort. The
following tips will help you achieve the best shave
possible, so your skin looks great on your wedding
day—and, of course, in all those photos thereafter.

- Before shaving, exfoliate. "Exfoliating" is
  sloughing off dead skin to make new,
  healthy skin glow, and there are various
  products on the market that will help you.
  Ask your fiancée—she's probably got one
  or two in her beauty bag. Typically you just
  massage the exfoliating lotion into your skin
  and rinse—the result is opened facial pores
  and the removal of dry, flaky skin—a perfect
  canvas for your upcoming shave.

- Sufficiently douse your skin with warm
  water. This will also help open pores and
  soften facial hair, for less irritation and razor
  burn. Steam and water from your pre-shave
  shower can help achieve sufficiently wet,
  warm skin.

- Thoroughly massage shaving cream into skin. This will allow the cream to better moisturize and take hold of stubble before you run your razor across it.

- Use a fresh blade. Dull, old blades are more apt to cause nicks and to irritate skin, because you'll have to use more pressure.

- Rinse your blade often. Don't allow shaving cream and stubble to build up on the blade.

- Use slow, short strokes. This will provide greater control over the area you're shaving, and less irritation.

- Shave with the grain. This means to shave in the direction that the hair is growing. When you shave in the opposite direction of hair growth, it causes irritation and the inevitable razor burn or nicked skin.

- Use moisturizer when you're finished shaving. You'll be amazed at how much better your skin will appear over time with the simple application of hydrating moisturizer, giving your skin more elasticity and a healthier-looking tone.

- If all these steps are too much for you, or you fear your wedding-day hands might be a little too jittery for a good, close shave, treat yourself to some old-fashioned grooming at your local barbershop. Call ahead of time to let him know it's your big day, so you won't have to wait. Take along Dad or your best man and treat them to a shave, too.

The Basics

Of course, a good shave isn't all you need to look your wedding-day best. In the months and weeks leading up to your wedding, follow these easy tips to ensure that you look like a million bucks:

- Use sunscreen. There's nothing wrong with a little tan, but be sure not to get sunburned, which can lead to unsightly peeling or even blistering.

- Avoid smoking and heavy drinking. Both take a toll on your looks, especially if you overindulge the night before the wedding. Prevent bloodshot eyes, pallid skin, and dark eye circles by drinking and smoking in moderation (or not at all).

- Exercise. The reasons are obvious—you'll be in better shape, have more energy, feel better, and look healthier.

- Drink lots of water. The recommended daily amount is eight 8-ounce glasses per day. In other words, a gallon. Seems like a lot, but water will give your skin a healthier appearance, it will make you feel fuller (and thus eat fewer cheeseburgers and chicken wings). Keep a water bottle at your workplace and get in the habit of sipping and refilling it numerous times during the day.

- Get enough sleep—especially the night before the wedding. You want to feel awake, vibrant, and clear headed for your big day.

- Eat properly. A nice healthy balance of carbs and proteins the morning of your wedding is the perfect meal—think two hard-boiled eggs with a slice of toast, or fruit and cottage cheese, or a bagel with cream cheese. Nothing too fatty or heavy, unless you want to feel a rock in your stomach as you recite your vows.

Perfect Hair

Hair is certainly not just the province of women, especially on your wedding day, when you're on full display. For the perfect wedding-day 'do, follow these simple steps:

- Don't wait until the day before your wedding to get a haircut. It's best to get it cut one to two weeks in advance, so hair has a chance to grow in a bit and lie more naturally. The only cure for a bad haircut is time.

- Get a sample haircut. If you're thinking of trying out a new style, do what brides have done for years—go in for a trial styling. This means some advance planning—if it's an extreme change, give yourself at least six months to allow mistakes to grow in. If there's not a drastic change in length and you'd simply like some help with a new style—say, a spiky look—make an appointment with a salon (ask your fiancée for recommendations) and have the stylist try some things out in advance. When the stylist has achieved the style you like, take a digital shot so that he or she can re-style it the same way on your wedding day—or practice in the weeks leading up to the wedding and style it yourself. Ask the stylist for product recommendations, too, so that you'll have the tools (gels, combs, etc.) to style it perfectly.

- Balding? Now might be the time to look into the hair replacement options you've always wondered about. Or to embrace your beautiful balding self. Just be sure to wear sunscreen ....

Hands

It doesn't matter if you work construction or in an office—chances are, the most effort you expend on your hands is the occasional obligatory fingernail clip. However, your fingernails are one of the most noticeable things about you—especially on your wedding day, when all attention will be on your new wedding ring. If you work in a profession that leaves your fingernails permanently dirty, or you've just neglected those ragged cuticles for too long, now is the time for a professional manicure. More and more men are taking advantage of this relatively inexpensive service (usually under $20) that brings amazing results.

With This Ring

Now to show off those well-groomed hands … choosing your wedding ring. If you thought your jewelry-buying days were over once you scored the engagement ring, think again. Not only do you have to buy her another ring, but you'll also have to pick one out for yourself. If you're not the jewelry-wearing type, the thought of wearing a ring might turn you off at first. But don't be surprised if your bride feels it's pretty important that you keep it on. After all, the ring is a symbol of one of the most important commitments you make in your lifetime. Just as you wish her to proudly wear her engagement and wedding rings, she wishes the same for you.

We know of one young gentleman who really hated wearing his wedding ring. Not only did the aesthetics offend him, but he also claimed it was uncomfortable and that exceptionally hearty hand-shakes actually hurt. So he decided to take matters into his own hands. One day he hid the ring in the pocket of an old pair of pants he never wore and told his bride, with a hangdog expression, that someone must have stolen it from his locker at the gym. He felt just terrible about it, he said. Although she wasn't pleased, she understood that such things happen, and they didn't replace it right away because of a temporary cash-flow issue. Six months later, while going through clothes to donate to the Salvation Army, she found the ring. The ensuing scene was not pretty.

The moral? Don't be sneaky. You'll get more lee-way on the ring issue, and many more like it, if you approach the conflict more directly.

Okay, now that we've established that you have to wear a ring, what type of ring will you choose? There are many more variations today than just the traditional plain band of gold. Some men choose white gold or platinum to match their bride's engagement and wedding ring. Some men choose rings with subtle patterns or cuts, which can add a more interesting flair. Also popular now are rings with two metals, such as yellow and white gold.

Etiquette dictates that your bride purchases your wedding ring, but we know that you'll probably want some input in choosing it. While you're at it, you should also choose a wedding ring for your bride, which you are responsible for purchasing. Your best bet is to consult with your original jeweler for a band style that will best complement the original engagement ring. If you've given her a traditional band with a solitaire diamond as an engagement ring, you can create a gorgeous com-bination with a complementary wedding ring.

Obviously, the wedding rings are crucial to the wedding ceremony. Your best man should guard them carefully prior to the ceremony so that they are not misplaced or forgotten on the wedding day.

While all this fussing and detail work about cloth-ing, hygiene, and jewelry may not be your usual style, they *are* important. After all, you don't want to look back on your pictures and video thinking how awful you look, or be stuck wearing a ring for life that you absolutely detest. An enthusiastic attitude and a little extra time spent can go a long way, whether you're choosing just the right wedding band or using hair gel for the first time.

I Hear Bells Ringing (Am I Hallucinating?)

In This Chapter

- Ensuring that everything's in order
- Pre-wedding activities to keep your mind occupied
- Tips for relieving wedding-related stress
- Surviving cold feet
- Wedding-day traditions
- Wedding-day etiquette

You've pored over the plans for months, discerning the best strategies to make this operation go smoothly. You've endured conflicts with underlings, peers, and superiors in your quest to make things right. The only thing left to do is wait and watch and hope that the operation goes smoothly and that there are few wedding-day casualties. It's D-Day, Colonel Commitment; read ahead for some wedding-day operatives that'll earn you your stripes.

Getting Your Ducks in a Row

The key to a successful wedding day is preparation, preparation, preparation. That means you've ensured that certain things are in order—well in advance of the big day. Though you may have gotten away with winging it in the past, this is not the day to tempt fate. Here are a few reminders of things to absolutely, positively make sure you have taken care of, prior to your wedding day.

Making It Legal

While a religious ceremony in front of hundreds of witnesses may feel like sealing the deal, in reality you have to take care of some legalities in advance. That means you must secure a wedding license before your wedding day—but not too far in advance, because marriage licenses expire after a relatively short period of time. Unless you're getting married in Las Vegas, where instant wedding licenses are de rigueur, you should acquire it far enough in advance to bridge any waiting-period dictates. Each U.S. state has different laws in place. And if you plan to marry abroad, each country has its own marriage laws to abide by. Check the laws in the region in which you plan to marry to be sure you're legally intact for the big day.

To get a license in most states, the bride and groom must show up in person at the county courthouse. You will be asked for current photo IDs and certified or notarized copies of birth certificates. If either party is divorced, you might need to bring a copy of the divorce decree or annulment; if one of you is widowed, a death certificate may be required. Call your local county courthouse in advance to determine exactly what you'll need.

Guard this license well, as you'll need it beyond your wedding day. If you are traveling out of the country or even on a short domestic flight, and you've booked your tickets as "Mr. and Mrs. Groom," you will need some sort of identification proving that the former Ms. Bride is now Mrs. Groom.

Don't Forget the Rings!

Between you and your best man, you should ensure that the wedding rings are ready and accounted for. That means confirming their readiness with the jeweler (give yourself at least a week's leeway to avoid undue stress), remembering to pick them up, and most important, ensuring that they're safely transported to the ceremony. With all that's on your mind, plan to delegate the final duty to your best man.

Writing Your Vows

Another wedding-day option that you and your bride might consider is writing your own vows, which can personalize your ceremony and make it a bit more unique. Obviously, this is one arena in which spontaneity is not particularly advised. Check with your wedding officiant as soon as you can to determine whether there are constraints or guidelines when writing vows of your own. If there are no constraints, here are a few guidelines to help you do it right:

- **Be personal.** This is the time to address your unique situation. Talk about the special things that made you fall in love with her, your views on the meaning of marriage, or your excitement about the future together. Sincerity and forethought go a long way.

- **Ask the right questions.** When contemplating the content of your vows, ask yourself about your unique situation and reflect on what this day—and your bride—really mean to you.

- **Keep them short.** Your vows don't have to be a thesis-worthy dissertation on commitment, love, and marriage. A few well-chosen anecdotes go much further than a full exposé of your innermost emotions.

- **Remember the seriousness of the event.** It's okay to be playful, but keep things on a relatively solemn level. This is not the time or place for embarrassing stories, intimate details, or references to the more basic aspects of marriage such as money and childbearing.

- **Practice, practice, practice.** Read your vows aloud in advance so that you're used to the nuances of your words. Be sure to bring a copy of them to your ceremony, or have the clergyperson read them for you and your bride to repeat. It's easy to forget even the most memorized of speeches under the stress of the occasion.

- **Print your vows in your program.** Sometimes it's difficult for everyone to hear the vows exchanged during the ceremony, especially if it's in a large or acoustically challenged venue. If you reprint them within your ceremony programs, you can be sure that everyone experiences them.

What Will You Do All Day?

If you're having a late-afternoon wedding, you will quickly learn the meaning of the word anticipation. Even if you do little else on a typical Saturday besides sleep and watch the prior week's worth of Tivo'd basketball games, you will find that having a lot of free time before your wedding is excruciating. First of all, you can't count on your betrothed for entertainment; she'll be MIA from sunup, doing things like her hair, her nails, and her makeup, which will take up her entire day. But you: Besides the few added maneuvers in hygiene discussed in Chapter 10, you will have nothing to fill your day from the moment you wake up to the time you put on your monkey suit.

So be sure to plan ahead. One organized groom with a 6:00 P.M. Saturday wedding decided to host all his groomsmen in a golf tournament. The two foursomes killed five full hours with 18 holes of golf and a pre-celebratory toast on the 19th—successfully and enjoyably filling the groom's whole day. Relaxing and therapeutic, the activity kept the groom's mind off the coming events.

Tired of living in a golfer's world? Yes, there are other activities to pass a summer day. (Though we challenge you to find one that kills as much time.) Whatever your sport—bicycling, running, basketball, tennis—just do it. The physical activity will relieve stress and tension and will give you something besides the wedding to focus on. Or if you find sports to be the most unrelaxing thing in the world, or it's the dead of winter, rent all three *Godfather*s with your best man, order some pizza, and set the alarm for shower time.

◁ Nuptial No-Nos

No matter what time you're getting married, get a good night's sleep before the wedding—especially if your rehearsal dinner is the night before. Even though you might be tempted to stay out late with your friends and family, you will be very unhappy if you have a hangover on your wedding day.

The point is to pursue some activity that won't have you ruminating about the events to come. If your idea of relaxing is having a few beers, heed this warning: A "few" is two or three over a couple of hours on a full stomach. On your wedding day, subtract one from that total. No one will be overly pleased with you if you show up buzzed to your own wedding. Besides, there's plenty of time for drinking right *after* the ceremony ....

The following are some stress-relief tips for your wedding day and beyond:

- Pursue physical activity. The endorphins released in your body have a positive physical effect on you, making you feel more confident, relaxed, and energized.

- If your mind is racing, pursue an activity that will distract you. Hang out with your best man and tell old stories. Play poker with your groomsmen. Rent a funny movie. Watch a sports event.

- Help your bride with last-minute finishing touches. If she's made some decorations herself, help put them up. If she and her family are doing any of the cooking, offer your assistance. Just don't see her in her dress ahead of time; it's supposed to be bad luck.

- Spend some time with your parents. They will appreciate the sentimentality of the moments just before their little boy becomes a man. Of course, if your parents have a tendency to drive you insane, do not add unnecessary stress to your day.

- Avoid excessive caffeine, alcohol, nicotine, and sugar. Too much of any of them, and you'll feel jittery or sleepy or you will crash from a sugar high.

- On the other hand, don't decide that this is the day you'll quit smoking.
- Read a good book.
- Meditate.
- Get a massage. If you've never had one, get over your fears. There is nothing more relaxing than a good full-body massage.
- Do some hard physical labor, such as moving furniture to your new house or putting up drywall. But don't do anything that might violate your physical integrity; we're thinking back injury, broken toe, sprained anything. Your bride might never forgive you for ruining the video by gimping down the aisle.

Icy Toes

It's natural for both men and women to experience "cold feet" immediately preceding their wedding. This is when you start violently doubting the wisdom of your idea to marry. Especially for men, it is quite normal; after all, it's going against the absolute fabric of masculinity to marry, violating traits such as independence and "playing the field." With all the pressure immediately preceding your ceremony, you might be inclined to doubt your decision. If this happens, get it off your chest—or just get over it. Your fears are being magnified by the intense pressure of the day. Unless you've come to a sudden epiphany backed up by solid evidence of wrongdoing by your fiancée, your feelings will be sure to fade once the pressure's off.

Groom Gambit

A strategy to follow if you get cold feet on your wedding day is this. Fill your mind with positive images of your bride—the time she took care of you when you were sick, how happy she was the day you proposed, how good she is with your nieces and nephews.

Wedding-Day Agenda

At your wedding, it's wise to set up some sort of day's agenda for you, your bride, and your close family members to know in advance. You should figure out timing; will there be a lag between the ceremony and reception for photos? If so, where will guests go in between? It's nice to avoid this lag if you can, but if constraints on your ceremony or reception site are tight, you might have to suck it up. For you and your wedding party, it'll probably mean a photo session—but with some tunes in the limo and a little celebratory champagne, you can start the party a little early. As for your guests, you might want to ask a close relative or friend to host a pre-wedding soirée where guests are welcome to hang out if they so desire. Or you might want to propose some options for activities—a nearby museum, coffeehouse, or park where they can take a walk.

Once you've arrived at the reception after the ceremony, there should be some sequence of events to move the night along. If you're having a fairly typical traditional wedding, that sequence consists of a receiving line, the introduction of the wedding party, a cocktail hour, dinner, and then dancing. Sprinkled within are the cake-cutting, a pre- or post-dinner toast from the best man and the bride's father, and the toss of the bouquet. You can include or subtract events, as well, depending on how you're structuring your party. Remember, it's your wedding. If you don't want to incorporate certain traditions, you don't have to.

Wedding Traditions

Speaking of those traditions … some are so ingrained in the institution of marriage that it would be difficult to break from them—such as the engagement ring or the wedding cake. But couples seem to be sloughing off other traditions, depending on their personal preferences, such as the receiving line and the bouquet toss. Your ethnic background, geographic region, and personal style will contribute greatly to these decisions. In the meantime, the following wedding traditions and their origins might help you decide.

The Honeymoon

It's doubtful that you'll want to break this particular tradition. But in fact, at one time honeymoons were anything but the blissful, romantic getaways they are today. The word comes from the early Christian era in Scandinavia, when men abducted women as brides from neighboring villages. The man and his bride would go into hiding for a period of time, during which their location was known only to the best man. They would remain in hiding until the bride's family ended its search for her; the couple would then return to the man's village.

A separate theory on the genesis of the honeymoon: Hundreds of years ago the bride's father would supply the groom with honey-mead—yesterday's version of Guinness Stout—for one month, or one moon, after the wedding. (Sure beats going back to work after two weeks.)

No matter which theory you adopt, a honeymoon is a great opportunity to kick back and relax after all the stress of wedding planning. Even if you only have a few days, a getaway with your new bride is something you'll always remember.

The Bouquet Toss

At its inception, the bouquet was a symbol of happiness. Somewhere along the way a tradition developed: to throw the bouquet over the bride's shoulder to an audience of unmarried or "unattached" women. Whoever catches the bouquet is said to be the next to marry. In recent years the bouquet toss has become less popular, possibly because it publicly delineates the attached women from the single women, which can be a touchy issue. Some women even take offense to this practice, believing that it symbolizes that they are incomplete without a man. Obviously these are all matters of opinion, and it is up to you as a couple to ultimately decide the bouquet-toss fate at your celebration. Harmless fun or anti-feminist? Only you can decide.

Throwing the Garter

At some weddings, throwing the garter goes hand-in-hand with tossing the bouquet. The garter is removed from the bride's leg by the groom (often to the tune of that old bawdy classic, "The Strip") and is then tossed over the groom's shoulder to a collection of unmarried men. The man who catches it then has to slide it up the leg of the woman who caught the bouquet, in front of a rowdy crowd of gawkers who will encourage him to go higher, higher, as the photographer snaps pictures of the whole event. The origin and meaning of this practice is unknown but in time may be credited to late-twentieth-century cheesiness.

The Chicken Dance

If you're hiring a disc jockey to play your music, you will probably be faced with the question: to chicken dance or not to chicken dance? (For those of you who are chicken-dance virgins, this is a special dance that's goofier than the hokey pokey and sillier than the Electric Slide, though similar in its group orientation and line-dance organization.) Those of our parents' generation seem to enjoy its wacky essence; in my cousin's wedding, this issue was a major point of contention between the bride and her father (One wanted it; one did not.) Once again, it's ultimately up to you.

Clink-of-Glass Smooching

Traditionally, the clinking sound of guests' silverware upon glassware during the reception dinner is a signal for the groom and bride to kiss. They clink, you kiss. There have been weddings where this has gotten out of hand, and the wedding couple barely has time to eat during an unreasonable number of requests. Don't feel that you must kiss just because you hear a clink. The clinker could be your smart-aleck nephew or perverted uncle—each of whom has his own agenda. Don't humor them more than you have to.

You may also wish to incorporate a new tradition that makes guests work a little harder for their reward. For instance, in place of glass-clinking, tell guests that you and the bride will kiss only if they approach your table to sing a song with the word "love" in the lyrics. Or if they tell a funny story about the bride or groom as children. You can be as creative as you like—simply have the best man or emcee announce your plan prior to the meal.

Wedding-Day Etiquette

All along, we've been saying it's your day, and you can do what you want. Now we're here to say it's your day—but to a limit. Obviously, this event revolves around you and your bride, and it's one of the more important occasions you'll experience in your lifetime. But you should also keep in mind that by having a wedding with invited guests, you are choosing to honor friends and family whom you'd like to share in the celebration.

That said, you should heed a few caveats in order to acknowledge your honored guests. The first, which is optional, is the receiving line. The *receiving line*, which can immediately follow the ceremony in church, or can reconvene at the reception site, consists of you, your bride, and both sets of parents, as well as bridesmaids and groomsmen if that is your wish. You can also limit attendants participating in your receiving line to the best man and maid of honor only.

Wedding Words _____

The **receiving line** is a convenient way to give a warm welcome to friends and family who've come to share your wedding.

If parents are divorced, you may choose to have fathers circulate among the guests instead of stand in line. If your father is hosting the wedding, however, you may want him to head the line anyway—simply separate divorced parents within the line to avoid confusion among guests. If you or your bride feels particularly close to stepparents, you may also ask them to receive.

The receiving line is meant to ensure that you have an opportunity to greet every guest at your wedding. After the ceremony or before the reception, guests will wait patiently in line to tell your bride how beautiful she looks, how happy they are for you, and how nice the ceremony was. (These are the three standard receiving "lines.") Some couples choose to eschew the receiving line because it takes a long time to greet every guest in this fashion, and it takes a real pro to make engaging small talk with up to a few hundred people in a row, one after the other. Not to mention that you must remember names.

Some couples instead choose to greet each table individually following dinner to ensure they haven't missed anyone. This process can go a little faster, and it happens at a time in the evening when everyone's a bit more relaxed. That can make for more meaningful exchanges.

Although you should make the most of enjoying your wedding, you should make some effort to greet and acknowledge all of your guests—not just your immediate family and friends.

Going the Extra Mile: Being a Hero

In This Chapter

- Romantic gestures
- Thanking your parents
- Remembering your wedding party
- Honoring your guests

Your engagement and wedding are the perfect time to fully display your metamorphosis from awkward adolescent to mature manliness. While being a groom in and of itself will be enough to make Great Aunt Dottie swoon, you can definitely go further during this time to create the stuff of family legend—stories that will even impress your grandchildren. Whether it's a grand gesture or a quiet consideration, there are ways you can go the extra mile during your wedding season, all of which are guaranteed to wow your bride, your groomsmen, your guests—or all of the above.

Grand Romantic Gestures

Sure, she already said "yes." But as the groom, you have tons of opportunity to make your wedding day extra-special for your bride. The following are some ideas that will impress her, and reconfirm that she's married the right guy, after all:

- Have flowers or a gift delivered the morning of the wedding. Be with her in spirit by sending a special delivery to her home as she gets ready, along with a personalized note. Her family and bridesmaids will ooh and aah over the romantic gesture.

- Write a special wedding-day toast or speech. Don't tell your fiancée that you've prepared something, but instead surprise her during toast-time with a few specially written words, just for her. She'll melt over the public declaration. Even better, if you're a musician, sing or play a special tune—with or without the band. Dedicate it to your lady. Watch the tears well up among the remainder of your female guests.

- Have your wedding-night accommodations prepared in advance. If you're staying at a hotel, ask if they will set up your room with candles, a warm bubble bath, rose-strewn sheets, or champagne and strawberries (or a heart-shaped pizza, if that's more your style). If you're staying in someone's home, or the hotel can't accommodate you, ask your best man or the maid of honor for help preparing your room for arrival. Your fiancée will love the romantic surprise.

- Start off your honeymoon in style. Hire a stretch limousine to take you to the airport, and see if you can finagle a special pass to your airline's first-class club so that you can wait for your flight in more comfort and less chaos. (Tell the airline it's your honeymoon—often an accommodating agent or airline employee will go the extra mile for the special occasion.)

Groom Gambit

A traditional all-woman shower offers the perfect PR opportunity for you, the groom. Arrange for flower bouquets to be delivered to your fiancée, her mother, and your mother; then show up at the tail end of the party to meet and greet the ladies and help pack up the car. (Two small gestures that can go a long way to impress.)

It's the Little Things ...

Sure, a grand gesture is memorable and will make for a fabulous story to tell all her friends and family. But sometimes it's the little, quiet things that make a big difference. Not to mention that they're good tactics to adopt for well beyond the engagement, too ...

- **Show some interest.** One of the biggest—and most easily preventable—mistakes that grooms make is displaying indifference. While most grooms won't be nearly as interested as their brides in every tiny detail of wedding planning—after all, how scintillating can choosing a cake frosting be?—try to muster up some enthusiasm from time to time. If you seem utterly disinterested in the planning, she'll take it personally and assume that you're not interested in her—or the marriage—either.

- **Take the initiative.** This goes a few steps beyond our first suggestion. Instead of waiting to be asked to pitch in for wedding-related duties, take on some tasks yourself. For instance, scout out bands or limousine companies to save the bride some legwork. Then come to her and report your findings—she'll be pleased and surprised, mark our words.

- **Be attentive.** Don't forget to steal a few moments alone with your bride at the wedding. You'd be surprised how distracting the party can be, especially in light of the fact that all the people you're closest to, from every facet of your life, will be in attendance. It's easy to forget what you're really there for—to celebrate your union with the bride. Show her some special attention.

- **Be a gentleman.** Whether your honeymoon finds you on the sassy streets of Paris or the skimpy beaches of South America, try not to ogle the other gorgeous women you'll inevitably encounter ... at least this one time.

Gift Ideas for Your Bride

Just when you thought the decision-making pressure was over—you bought the engagement ring and wedding ring and you've settled all the wedding-day details—you realize that you must pick out *another* gift for the bride. But what should this gift entail? After all these expenses, is another gift absolutely necessary? If you agree in advance not to exchange gifts, it's certainly not mandatory. But if you'd like to mark the occasion with another special remembrance—and make (another) decidedly romantic gesture—you might want to think about surprising your bride with a gift, such as the following:

- Jewelry, especially jewelry she can wear on her wedding day.
- A hobby-related gift. This should be based on her specific interests, such as, say, new equipment for rock climbing or new supplies for scrapbooking.
- A household gift. (This doesn't mean a toaster—unless you know she really truly wants one.) Try something more like a unique piece of artwork or a great antique.

- Giftware, such as a beautiful vase or clock from Tiffany's. Or a splurge item from her favorite specialty store.

- Luxurious, expensive lingerie. (A gift for the both of you.)

- Spa treatments.

- Tickets to a special vacation destination for your first anniversary.

- Something handmade or homemade that uses your talent and/or skills, whether you're a writer, artist, carpenter, or gardener.

Thanking Your Parents

Whether they've contributed their finances or their time (or just their egg and sperm), it's awfully nice to show appreciation for all your parents have done this wedding season. Some gift ideas include flowers to arrive when you're already gone on your honeymoon; a gift certificate to their favorite restaurant, so that they can finally relax with a dinner on you; spa treatments or massages; hobby-related gifts, such as a tennis racket, golf clubs, or an item to add to a special collection; a gift certificate to an inn or hotel to spend some time away together; tickets to a show or concert they'd enjoy; a framed picture of you and them from the wedding or a special wedding "parent's album"; even a card expressing your thanks.

It's easy to get caught up in yourselves and the occasion; show your parents that they raised you right with a token of your appreciation for all they've done.

Remembering Your Wedding Party

In the worst of situations, bridesmaids and grooms-men can end up feeling like unpaid extras when it comes to wedding participation. Why? In the frenzy of wedding planning, the bride and groom often make demands and give orders as if they were hired help rather than honored participants. We know you wouldn't dream of doing that, but it bears remembering that these people may have made some sacrifices to take part in your wedding. Not only can it become a sizeable investment, between the cost of buying or renting wedding attire, hosting parties, and travel and lodging costs for your events ... but they've also given their time and attention to create the best day possible for you and your bride.

At the wedding itself, be sure to acknowledge each member of your wedding party by name, thanking them for their help and support. Don't forget to have the photographer take a picture of you and your bride, together with your wedding party, and consider sending them each a copy of the photo following the wedding. You may also wish to include fun, detailed profiles of each bridesmaid and groomsman in your ceremony program, so that guests understand their connection to you and their honored status at the wedding.

> 👍 **Groom Gambit** _____
>
> Groomsman gifts don't have to be
> expensive to be meaningful. In fact, try to
> opt for something original—and something
> the boys will really appreciate. While
> you'll see countless baubles like beer steins
> and cigar holders hawked on Internet
> sites, consider giving something more
> unique, or something they can really use:
> an elegant set of poker chips, or tickets to
> a sporting event or concert, for instance.

In addition, offering a thoughtful gift to each
member of your wedding party is a popular traditional gesture. (See Appendix B for some gift
ideas.) You and your bride may also wish to host
a post-wedding get-together for everyone to show
your appreciation. Whether you host a home party
or spring for tickets to a special concert or event, it
will give everyone the chance to reunite and remi-
nisce in a fun, relaxed setting.

Honoring Your Guests

With few exceptions, people love weddings.
Why? Weddings hold something for everyone.
Whether it's tasty food, free booze, good music,
or unchecked optimism, all but the most cynical
scrooges can find something to enjoy.

While this day is certainly meant for you and your bride, it's also meant for your guests to enjoy. And the happier your guests are, the more fun your celebration will be. Therefore it can be worthwhile to incorporate some special strategies to make guests feel as if they are truly honored. That's the theory behind the best hotels and restaurants, and it's the secret held by the world's best party planners. Here are some ideas to make your guests feel extra special.

Including Them in Weekend-Long Plans

Many wedding guests today are required to travel to far-flung destinations to attend a wedding. If you're inviting a lot of out-of-towners, ensure that you make it worth their while. In addition to immediate family and the wedding party, be sure to invite all out-of-town guests to the rehearsal dinner. And because this is, in essence, a vacation weekend for them, organize or suggest activities in which they can take part during nonwedding festivities. Many weekend-long weddings will include afternoon pool parties, tours to nearby attractions, spa or golf outings, or post-wedding brunches to ensure as much together-time with guests as possible. This also serves to make out-of-town guests feel included and happy to have come the distance. Feel free to include in-town guests in any activities you wish, as well.

Creating Guest Baskets

Another special treat for out-of-town guests is to create a welcome basket to greet them when they arrive in town. This is an especially nice touch if they're checking into a hotel for the weekend. In your basket, include items that will make their stay a little easier—bottled water, snacks, a small sewing kit, bubble bath—personalize it any way you wish. Be sure to also include a welcoming note from you and the bride, as well as an agenda for the weekend's events, if you wish.

Greeting Your Guests

At the rehearsal dinner and at the wedding, be sure to personally greet and chat with as many guests as possible. This is a small measure that can make guests feel a sense of inclusion and honor.

Including Guests in Photos, Toasts, or Slide Shows

Some families put together slide shows or photo albums for display at the rehearsal dinner and/or wedding. If you plan to do this, make an effort to include as many of your invited guests as possible in your display.

Writing Sincere Thank-You Notes

Acknowledging your guests should also extend to post-wedding activity. Yes—it's the dreaded thank-you notes. If writing a thank-you note for

Aunt Millie's annual birthday gift has given you trouble over the years, this task might cause you some trepidation (think Aunt Millie times 200). It is proper etiquette, however, to write half the thank-you notes yourself for wedding gifts you receive as a couple.

Thank-you notes can be ordered with the rest of your stationery (invitations, place cards, and so on). You might get a better deal this way, in volume. Plus, you'll have them on hand immediately following the wedding. Some couples take thank-you cards to write on their honeymoon flight—especially if there's a long trip involved. This way, you can get it out of the way immediately and kill some boring flight time with a practical purpose.

Thank-you notes should be handwritten and acknowledge the specific gift you've received and how you'll use it. For example, if you've received a skillet, talk about how you can't wait to use it to make Saturday brunch for your bride. If it's 1 of 12 place settings, mention how you're looking forward to entertaining. In other words, phrase the note in such a way that it makes the giver feel good about what he or she's given.

Send thank-you notes out as soon as possible. Especially if the giver has ordered your gift from a registry—and the store is sending it out directly—he or she has no way of knowing that it actually arrived at your doorstep until a thank-you note confirms it.

If the idea of writing 100 thank-you notes makes you break out in hives, delegate this task to your bride through the power of negotiation. Offer her something in return for doing all of them; then, you can just sign them at the end. Although it is proper etiquette for the groom to write half of them, it's a safe bet that most guests won't be surprised to receive a thank-you note in the bride's handwriting. Then, you get what you want, your bride gets something she wants—and everyone is happy. If you become stuck with the task, however, simply refer to Appendix C so that you can be sure you're doing it right.

Chapter 13

Real Grooms, Real Stories

In This Chapter

- Imbibing on your wedding day
- Irresponsible wedding-day behavior
- The groom who did it all
- Speaking up on your bride's behalf
- The groom who did it without his parents' blessing
- Ready for monogamy

Suddenly, you feel so alone. Before you were engaged, it seemed as if all your friends were getting married; now it seems as if they're all swinging singles. You have concerns, hopes, and fears, but you can't talk to any of your guy friends about them—and your bride-to-be would freak out if she knew some of the things on your mind. You're afraid this unusual pre-marriage state of mind will begin affecting your behavior and that it will come out on your wedding day. We're here to tell you you're not alone. Plenty of grooms have experienced wedding-day jitters and mishaps.

Learn from them to avoid your own wedding disasters. Here are their stories.

The Groom Who Drank Too Much

A groom from Memphis, Tennessee, was engaged to be married to the girl of his dreams. He was a country-music producer; she was a kindergarten teacher. They had met at the large southern state college they both attended, where he worshipped her for three years before she even knew he existed. When he finally got up the courage to introduce himself, they became virtually inseparable. At college he had been a football player and she had been president of her sorority. Both high achievers and plugged in socially, this couple worked hard and played hard. Since their college days, however, neither of them partied much anymore. They had careers to keep them busy and each other to keep them happy.

Along came their wedding day and the groom was nervous—not because he thought he was making a mistake, but because he hated being in the spotlight. Their wedding guest list numbered a hefty 400 people, many of whom he did not know. The thought of making small talk in a receiving line with so many people put him into a cold sweat. The thought of standing and speaking at the altar in front of them actually made him light-headed. He consulted his best man for advice as he dressed for the wedding.

His best man, a football-player buddy from college, had just the solution. He pulled out a flask and encouraged the groom to take a sip to calm his nerves. Unfortunately, the groom went too far and finished off the flask, only to remember he hadn't eaten anything that day. But hey, he felt great! Of course, today he knows he won't be watching his wedding video again any time soon—seeing himself stumble on his way up to the altar was a one-time viewing only. And he wishes he remembered more of the ceremony and reception. So does his bride.

Nuptial No-Nos

Take it easy on the spirits before and during your wedding festivities—you don't want the "happiest day of your life" to be the one you don't remember. If you're nervous before the wedding, try some natural relaxation techniques—deep breathing, meditating, exercise, or a distracting activity. Lay off the liquor until you're already married.

The Groom Who Drank Too Little

Alison fell in love with her groom in New York City because he was very sensible and serious, not like the "boys" she encountered at the bars her friends liked to go to. He had put himself through college and law school on his own, secured a position at one of the better firms in the city, and devoted himself to a career. He was the type of guy who does what he says he's going to do— friends can always rely on him, and he calls his mother regularly. So when it came to his wedding, he helped his bride plan much of it so that the burden didn't fall solely on her, and he worried over the details almost as much as she did. "Were all the responses received? Has the band gotten the playlist yet? Are our honeymoon reservations confirmed?" Okay, some might call him anal. His bride called him Andy.

On his wedding day, Andy was well prepared. His tuxedo fit like a tapered glove, his week-old haircut had grown out just enough, and he managed to shave with no nicks. He arrived at the church not on time, but early. He watched from the vestibule as the guests arrived, worrying that he wouldn't get to talk to all of them. When he greeted his bride as she met him at the end of the aisle, the ceremony went off without a hitch.

 Groom Gambit

> Don't forget to enjoy your wedding! Don't get caught up in the "obligation" portion of the wedding, forgetting to whisk off the bride every so often for a dance or a stolen kiss. Don't let the evening end before it's even really begun.

And so did the reception. But the bride soon realized that "no hitches" and "fun" were not necessarily synonymous. In fact, she barely spent time with her groom all evening. Andy was busy making sure he greeted and conversed meaningfully with each and every person. Now, there's nothing wrong with being polite, she thought, but polite to a fault was a problem. She only danced two songs with him, and she knew he didn't relax and enjoy the fruits of their laborious planning all evening. The bottom line? She knew he'd be a good provider, but he might need loosening up a bit on the social side.

The Groom Who Didn't Show Up

Tom and Laurie were in love. Or so Laurie thought. They had met through mutual friends and dated for two years before Tom asked her to marry him, after a little encouragement (a.k.a.: ultimatum) from Laurie. During the year-long engagement, Tom found himself voluntarily on the planning sidelines, while Laurie and her mother planned the royal wedding: hundreds of guests, white tie, multiple ice sculptures, tulips flown in directly from Holland. In other words, the wedding Laurie had always dreamed of flaunting in her friends' faces.

Tom had little to say but did as he was told. He bought his tuxedo. He planned a three-week honeymoon to the South Pacific islands. And a subconscious nagging slowly evolved into outright wonderment as to why he had ever thought Laurie was his soulmate. She bossed him around. His friends couldn't stand her. And she cared less about him, he knew, than his year-end bonus.

But Tom thought it was too late to back out. After all, the wedding was planned. The announcement had appeared in the newspaper. Guests had bought their plane tickets. There was nothing he could do now except make the best of an unfortunate situation.

But when he woke up on his wedding day soaked with sweat and remembered his dream of Laurie turning into a wolf and trying to eat him alive, he knew he couldn't go through with it. So he didn't. He simply took the plane ticket, called his best man, and treated him to a trip to Bora Bora.

Nuptial No-Nos

If you're not sure you've made the right decision, confide in a close friend. You're probably just having cold feet, which happens to the best of grooms on their wedding days. But by all means, don't stiff your bride at the altar.

Now, gentlemen—we don't recommend trying this at home, as it is extremely dangerous. While he was away, most of his earthly goods were destroyed, though he was never able to prove to authorities that it was Laurie who did it. Plus,

500 wedding guests think he's a total loser. The bottom line? If you're going to cancel your wedding, give some advance warning. Whether you're justified or not, canceling at the last minute is simply bad form.

The Groom Who Did It All

Between Josh and Suzanne, Josh was the organized one. To Josh, clutter and disorganization were the enemy, so he generally established the plans in their relationship. For example, when he proposed, he created a "scavenger hunt" for Suzanne, with a series of clues she had to follow all over their small town in order to find him waiting with the engagement ring. His game was so extravagant that it took her more than two hours to finish it, whereby he drove her into the nearest city to have dinner and a romantic getaway at one of the nicest hotels in town. Now, this kind of proposal takes patience and hard work, which Josh had in abundance.

Wedding Words

A **control freak** is a person who cannot allow any decision to be made without his or her say-so. Even if your bride is doing much of the planning but you feel compelled to give the final stamp of approval on every little detail, you qualify. Trust your bride. She may actually have a worthy opinion.

When it came time to plan the wedding, Josh was eager and willing to take on the task. Though his friends couldn't figure out why he'd ever get involved in more than he was forced to, Josh felt compelled to find the best vendors at the lowest prices, which took some serious legwork. At first, Suzanne was pleased with the arrangement, but then she began to resent her exclusion from her own wedding plans—especially when Josh began questioning any choices she *did* make. After all, wasn't she the one who was supposed to be making these decisions? It came to the point where she began to resent decisions she would have normally supported, simply because he was taking over. She began wondering whether Josh was a *control freak* who would need to take charge of everything for the rest of their lives.

The moral—you can't control everything. Even if you try, you'll end up attracting a lot of resentment. Begin developing decision-sharing habits now with your bride that will last a lifetime.

The Groom Who Married Without His Parents' Blessing

David and Kristen were like two peas in a pod. They both loved to ski, they wouldn't miss a Chicago Bears game, and neither of them could get enough Thai food. They were meant for each other.

Except for one little factor. David was Jewish, and Kristen was Catholic. Neither set of parents approved of the fact that they were dating, even though they thought highly of the individuals. When they became engaged, however, all hell broke lose.

David's parents tried to stop the wedding any way they could. They threatened to lock him up or disown him (melodrama was a family trait). When it came down to it, though, David wouldn't budge. He loved Kristen, and he knew that they would work hard to raise their children to learn both faiths, but more important, to be good people. So they eloped, and broke the news to both sets of parents when they returned home.

Though his parents weren't happy at first, they faced the inevitable and eventually lightened up. They now accept Kristen in their lives, and actually threw a post-wedding reception for the couple a few months later, introducing the couple to friends and family—the ultimate acceptance.

Of course, this level of acceptance may not always be the case. Be sure to consider this conflict—and how you'll handle it—very carefully before deciding to wed.

 Groom Gambit

Tread carefully when it comes to interfaith romances. What your parents seem cool about today might change drastically once you're engaged. Diplomacy is the key to harmony, and don't give up on your parents.

The Groom Who Never Spoke Up

Chloë was a strong woman. That's what Burt found so attractive about her. Chloë was a woman who knew what she wanted and when she wanted it, and she wasn't brash or rude about it. In fact, she was one of the most diplomatic people Burt had ever met.

Burt recognized that maybe this attraction was somewhat Freudian in nature. His mother, too, was quite headstrong—she'd had to be, as a corporate lawyer in New York City. She was also quite involved in her children's lives—she was a disciplinarian, a confidante, and a trouble-shooter all wrapped into one. It was no wonder that when Burt announced he was getting married, it was all she could do to resist taking a leave of absence to help plan the wedding.

Chloë, of course, had her own ideas. She had envisioned almost every aspect of her wedding for many years, and already knew the venue, the flowers, the music, and the cake she wanted. Not to mention that her own mother had some ideas, too. So when her future mother-in-law began making request after request to change various aspects of the wedding, in a decidedly unsubtle way, Chloë began getting frustrated.

It came to a head when her mother, who was trying to plan a shower, presented Burt's mother with a list of three different days they could have it, based on a number of considerations including the bridesmaids' schedules, as well as her own. When

Burt's mother insisted that none of these dates would do because they interfered with her tennis schedule, Chloë decided she had had enough. She called on Burt to put his mother in her place. After all, it was their wedding, and Chloë's parents were paying for it.

But Burt wouldn't say boo. He refused to get in the middle, which only incited Chloë more. Finally the normally diplomatic Chloë hashed it out with her future mother-in-law in a phone call that both of them would like to forget. After that, mom-in-law kept a much lower profile, but the tension remained well past the wedding day.

 Groom Gambit

> Don't wuss out on your bride, especially during this stressful time. Any mother-in-law knows that the less she has to say about her son's wedding plans, the better. If she insists on being overly opinionated, it's up to you to diplomatically intervene to prevent unnecessary long-term conflict between your bride and your mother.

The Groom Who Wasn't Ready for Monogamy

For his whole life, Phillip had never wanted for anything—his grandfather's successful company had made life very comfortable for the family. He had grown up on a 25,000-acre horse ranch outside of Dallas, been schooled in the best New England boarding schools, spent his summers in Europe, and was accepted into Yale despite his less-than-stellar grades, as his dad was an alumnus.

When Phillip met Cassandra at Yale, he thought she resembled a modern-day Grace Kelly—and so did everyone else. She was from a "good" family herself; he laid on the full-court press until she succumbed. They became the golden couple at Yale, and everyone wondered how far from perfect their children could actually end up.

The years went on; Phillip finished business school, and finally proposed to Cassandra. She delightedly accepted, quickly beginning her plans by asking 11 of her closest friends to be bridesmaids. At the time, she did not know that one would betray her.

Phillip, in the meantime, had gotten bored with Cassandra. He began drinking and carousing until all hours at Manhattan bars and clubs while Cassandra planned the wedding. When he ran into Lily one night, her maid-of-honor, he realized he had never noticed how attractive she really was. We'll spare you the rest of the lurid details.

As we're all aware, in a group of friends it's tough to keep a secret. Cassandra found out the bad news at the wedding reception, when a concerned friend thought she ought to know before it was too late (why she hadn't told her three hours before is anyone's guess). Regardless, after a few glasses of wine, Cassandra decided it was time everyone knew, and she broke the news in front of much of Manhattan/ Dallas society. Needless to say, Cassandra's dad has made it difficult for Phillip to eat lunch in that town again.

___◁│ **Nuptial No-Nos** _____

> As any man with a brain knows, stay away from the maid-of-honor. (It's much too close to home.) Of course, the real moral is that if you're not ready to be monogamous, then simply don't get married. You'll save everyone a lot of grief in the long run.

The Groom Who Did His Best

Inevitably, you will run into some type of problem during the planning and execution of your wedding. These grooms' stories are only meant to illustrate that the better the planning, diplomacy, and behavior, the more successful your wedding and ensuing marriage will be. The key is making the stuff within your control go smoothly, because there's enough already out of your control to send you for a tailspin. In other words, don't create your own problems. And our most important advice yet? Hang on to your sense of humor. If ever you needed it, it's now.

Wedding Resources

With the incredible number of wedding-related sites online, it's almost impossible to consider what people did before life on the World Wide Web. There is an endless number of general wedding sites online, boasting information ranging from etiquette to registry services to ideas for flowers, photography, video, favors, and so on. They all have one thing in common—heavy support from advertisers and online merchants who sponsor and link to these sites hoping for e-commerce. Clearly, these merchants' wishes are coming true because there is no dearth of advertisers or retailers hawking their wares.

Finding wedding sites is as easy as going to any search engine, typing in "weddings," and waiting for the results. But to make your life easier, here are a number of quick tips to get you on your way.

General Sites

www.groomsonline.com

A comprehensive resource directed specifically toward grooms, this site offers information about topics ranging from the bachelor party to gifts to honeymoon planning.

www.theknot.com

One of the best, most comprehensive wedding websites. Nicely designed, with articles covering almost every conceivable wedding-related topic. There's even a relatively comprehensive section for grooms (but of course, you won't need that after finishing this book …).

www.marthastewart.com

Yes, Martha's empire is still going strong post-incarceration. And, as in her magazine, beautiful photography and tasteful ideas for weddings rule this site. If the aesthetic side of you is crying out, this site's for you. Our little secret.

Registry Sites

www.thebigday.com

Totally cool site that enables you to register your honeymoon online, for goodies ranging from flights to hotels to in-room massages to breakfast in bed. The site breaks down big-ticket items, such as flights, into gift-sized portions (e.g., a $1,000 flight is divvied up into ten $100 gifts). Definitely check this one out.

www.bloomingdales.com

The quintessentially stylish department store also offers an online registry.

www.target.com

Previously, you had to register for Target's "Club Wedd" goodies in-store only. But now you can do it online, too. You may decide you'd rather see everything in person first, however. When you get to the store, all you need to do is sign in, get a bar scanner, and go nuts; all your gift choices are automatically entered into the computerized system once you "zap" them with the scanner. Target offers affordable appliances and household items in very cool designs that you can't find anywhere else, thanks to the talented contributions of designer Michael Graves. Which means you've got some tough—but fun—choices to make. The website is chock full of info, helping you to manage your list and enabling your guests to order from your registry online—saving them a trip to the store.

Honeymoon/Travel Sites

If you like to surf the Net, fewer industries will give you more options than the travel biz. Honeymoon planning is just a subset of the industry. The Internet is a great place to start for ideas on where to go and a quick lesson on how much it will cost you. You can book your vacation directly online, but be extremely careful that you're dealing with a reputable company. FYI—the following sites are not necessarily recommended by this book; we just found them online the same way you'd find them, and we're just reporting on our legwork. So tread carefully in all your online dealings.

What's great about the web is that the information is there to find if you want to use it for price comparisons when dealing with travel agents. Keep in mind that travel agents will do a little more of the homework for you and presumably have a level of expertise and knowledge that will add value to your overall vacation. If all else fails, don't forget your local bookstore, which carries hundreds of travel books that you can buy and take with you. Fodor's guides are particularly good for the inside scoop.

www.travelzoo.com

This is a terrific site that compiles a daily list of the best travel deals out there, ranging from airfares to cruises to hotel stays. They also offer a weekly newsletter that's fun to browse for specific deals and dates that suit your needs.

www.usabride.com

Click on "honeymoons" and you'll find honeymoon destination information and packages worldwide, ranging from the United States to the Caribbean to Europe and much more.

www.honeymoonsinc.com

This site features mostly "first class" all-inclusive packages such as Sandals, Couples, and SuperClubs resorts at "high-volume" discounts.

www.unforgettablehoneymoon.com

Another site dedicated mostly to honeymoon packages, this site offers moderate to five-star level packages.

www.orbitz.com

A comprehensive travel-planning site that includes flights, hotels, and packages, and also claims to offer the most low airfares around.

www.cheaptickets.com

More than its name implies, this site also offers everything from flights, hotels, vacation packages, and last-minute specials in all price ranges.

www.expedia.com

Similar to Orbitz, this is another comprehensive site that offers up the most competitive prices on airfare, rental cars, and hotels from select providers.

Don't forget to check the major discount airlines, such as Southwest and JetBlue, for great deals on airfare if you book in advance. Go to www.southwest.com or www.jetblue.com for details.

Gifts Online

It's difficult to swing the proverbial dead cat around on the Web and not be barraged with vendors trying to sell wedding wares. To find gifts for your groomsmen, type in "groomsman gifts" into any search engine, and watch the possibilities arise.

B

Gift-Giving Guide

It's probably pretty obvious to you by now that exchanging gifts is a large part of the wedding tradition (and to some, unfortunately, the whole point). Not only will you receive gifts—and probably a lot of them—but you will also be responsible for choosing some—for your bride, your best man, your groomsmen, and your parents. These gifts should be chosen with care; you should pick items with sentimental or lasting value. In other words, a bottle each of Wild Turkey for your groomsmen ain't gonna cut it.

To help you along with gift ideas for all the important people in your life, here's a quick referral guide in a range of budgets and styles to suit any groom. If the money's just not there after all the wedding expenses, a card with some special words that arrives the morning of your wedding will do nicely.

Gifts for the Bride

- Jewelry, especially jewelry she can wear on her wedding day. A lovely strand of pearls, pearl or sapphire earrings (something blue), a delicate platinum bracelet—anything goes. She will probably plan ahead what jewelry she's wearing on her wedding day, so you might want to give her your special gift a little early—or prep her that something might be on its way. You can also get her something to wear after the wedding. You know her preferences best, so choose something that she can keep forever.

- Something related to a hobby. If she's an avid reader, find a limited, antique, or signed edition of a book by her favorite author. If she paints, get her the upscale brush set she's always wanted but has been too practical to splurge on. A skier might want a new pair of parabolic skis. Whatever her hobby, get something that has meaning and something that will have lasting value.

- Something for the house. Maybe it's an original piece of artwork. An antique vanity table. A pretty window box for flowers. Heck, even a dishwasher. Basically, choose anything that will add beauty and make her life easier.

- Giftware, such as a beautiful vase or clock from Tiffany's. Or a splurge item from her favorite specialty store.

- Spa treatments.
- Tickets to a special vacation destination for your first anniversary.
- Something handmade or homemade. If you're a writer or artist, create something original to honor the day. If you're great with your hands, build a rocking chair or table. Plant her a garden that will bloom year after year. Extra points count for originality and creativity.
- A monthly bouquet of flowers. Online clubs and florists market special plans where you can pre-order and pre-pay for flowers to arrive on your doorstep at regular intervals, such as every month for a year. Drop hints that you'd like the similarly designed beer-of-the-month membership.
- Gifts related to specific interests:
  - **Cooking.** Gourmet cookware or a set of great cookbooks
  - **Gardening.** Good quality gardening tools. Have them engraved with her new initials
  - **Antique collecting.** An antique lamp, table, or other piece from her favorite era
  - **Sports or working out.** A home step machine, treadmill, or weight set, inline skates, or equipment related to her favorite sport (a snow board, waterskis, surf board, etc.)

- **Reading.** Membership in the literary guild or book-of-the-month club, or a book of love poems
- **Tennis.** New racquet or a club membership for both of you
- **Skiing.** A cute ski-bunny outfit you'd love to see her wear, or new skis
- **Travel.** Plane tickets for a future trip, or reservations at an out-of-town bed and breakfast
- **Golf.** New clubs, a new bag, or a club membership
- **Writing.** Elegant stationery, a silver pen, or a laptop computer
- **Movies.** Limited-edition, signed movie poster; a DVD player; or a home theater
- **Collecting.** A rare or hard-to-find collectible
- **Art or home crafts.** Lessons or supplies
- **Spectator sports.** Hockey, football, or basketball season tickets (Lucky guy.)
- **Driving.** A remote starter for her car, a car CD player, or, if you've got the bucks, a new car
- **Education.** First-year tuition or money toward classes
- **Pretty things.** A music or jewelry box, a ring holder, crystal candlesticks, or a vase (although you might receive a lot of these types of items as wedding gifts)

- **Work.** A weekend getaway, a day-spa certificate, or a pre-paid massage from a top salon
- **Practicality.** A needed item for your home such as a couch, table, bedroom or dining set
- **Nightlife.** Dinner at the most expensive or exclusive restaurant in town for your six-month anniversary
- **You.** Luxurious lingerie

Gifts for Groomsmen

It is standard to honor your groomsmen with a special gift close to your wedding date, as thanks for standing by you during your special time. How much you spend is wholly up to you (you might not have much left in your budget after all the wedding expenses), but grooms have been known to spend anywhere from $20 to $100 (or more) per gift. As you can see, this expense can quickly add up, especially if you have a large wedding party. Don't go totally on the cheap; you want to get a gift that will stand the test of time. But you also don't have to break the bank to buy a tasteful, worthwhile gift. You don't have to choose identical gifts for each groomsmen, either; in fact, it's proper to give your best man something a little extra. Here are some ideas for the entire wedding party:

- A silver Swiss Army knife—unless your guys are prone to violence
- A watch. You'll have to splurge a little to get decent ones.
- A glass or silver beer stein or flask. Unless your guys have been in rehab (or should be).
- A humidor or cigar cutting set. Or a box of Cubans, if you can get them.
- Zippo lighters in gold or silver or a unique design
- A silver or gold pen set
- A business-card holder. Job required.
- A picture frame
- A barbecue set
- An engraved travel mug
- A money clip
- Cuff links or tuxedo studs
- A mini travel bar
- An old-fashioned shaving set
- A wooden dresser-top box for cuff links and tux studs
- A leather shaving bag with initials
- A wine-stopper set
- Silver or leather key rings
- Golf-related gifts
- Gifts from a specialty store, such as a clock in an original design or a chess set

- A portable CD player with individual CDs according to the groomsmen's tastes
- A fun gadget from a store such as The Sharper Image or Hammacher Schlemmer. Think massager, electronic organizer, or golf net for home chipping.
- Sports tickets for a future game, to which you can all go together
- A special or limited-edition hardcover book
- Suits. Subsidize their purchase instead of asking groomsmen to wear rented tuxes
- Great silk ties they can wear on the day of the wedding.

Gifts for Parents

Although it's not mandatory, it is awfully nice to acknowledge both sets of parents with a gift following your wedding. Here are some ideas:

- Flowers to arrive while you're on your honeymoon. Nothing says "thank you" like flowers.
- A gift certificate to their favorite restaurant, where they can finally relax with a dinner on you
- Spa treatments. (You'll know whether your father would actually go for that.)
- A gift certificate to an inn or hotel to spend some time away together

- Tickets to a show or concert they'd enjoy
- A framed picture of the four of you from the wedding
- A special wedding "parent's album"
- A simple card expressing your thanks

Writing Thank-You Notes They'll Remember

If you've ever received a thank-you note, you'll understand the subtle difference between one written out of duty and one that has a little more sentimental value. The former sounds like something your mother dictated to you in fifth grade to thank Aunt Mabel for a birthday present; the latter makes a more personal statement.

There's no time like your wedding to learn the difference. Naturally, when you're writing hundreds of thank-you notes in a single sitting, they tend to fall more in the cookie-cutter range than in the homemade apple-pie category. This little guide, however, will give you a few tips on writing a proper and well-mannered thank-you note that allows your personality and sincerity to come through.

Here is an example of the fifth-grade-level thank-you letter:

> Dear Aunt Mable,
>
> Thank you dearly for the ceramic ashtray. Your kind gesture means a great deal to us.
>
> Love,
> Billy

There are a number of things lacking in this letter. The first is any kind of sincerity or personal touch. Even if Billy hates the gift, he should attempt to make some sort of sincere statement about it, such as "It is unique and unusual, and will be a nice addition to our patio." Aunt Mabel's name is also misspelled, which is inexcusable. (If you're unsure of spellings, consult with your mother or another person in the know.)

The following letter illustrates what you should be aiming for in your thank-you notes:

> Dear Aunt Mabel,
>
> Thank you so much for the beautiful silver candelabra. Jody and I have already found a place for it in our new house, on the mantel above the fireplace. A decorator couldn't have found a more perfect piece for the space!
>
> We were so honored you could travel to town for our wedding, and Jody particularly enjoyed meeting you. Can't wait for you to visit next time you're in town.

Talk to you soon.

Love,
Billy and Jody

The bottom line? When writing a thank-you note, pay close attention to the following points:

- Double-check the spelling of the person's name.

- Use your own language, as if you were speaking face-to-face.

- Match up the gift with the giver (be sure to keep meticulous records of who gave you what gift—you will never remember otherwise).

- Mention how you'll use the gift.

- Include a personal message about your happiness at seeing the recipient of the letter at the wedding. Or express your regret that he or she was unable to attend.

- The note should include the signatures of both you and your bride.

You may want to choose thank-you notes with your initials or a unique design. You can order note cards when you order your wedding invitations and RSVP cards. You may get a more reasonable package deal that way.

Top-Ten Things to Remember on Your Wedding Day

10. **Eat.** If you're having a buffet or food stations at the reception, it may be difficult to tear yourself away from guests and/or the dance floor. In this case, ask your best man in advance to make you a plate.

9. **Greet your guests.** Have a receiving line, or greet guests at each table individually. You don't have to have an in-depth conversation with every single guest, but it is polite to try to greet as many guests as possible.

8. **Dance.** Don't get so caught up in conversation that you forget to let off a little steam on the dance floor.

7. **Have fun.** You and your families have put a lot of time, effort, and money into the celebration of this union. Make the most of it and enjoy yourself.

6. **Take note of photo opportunities.** Make sure someone takes photos of all close family and friends, especially grandparents, children, out-of-town friends and family, and your entire immediate family.

5. **Thank your parents.** More than likely, they've gone out of their way to help give you this wedding (not to mention raised you from birth). Be sure to express your appreciation.

4. **Spend time with out-of-town guests.** You'll have friends and family at your wedding whom you see all the time, so make sure to spend enough time with friends and family you don't see as often.

3. **Don't drink and drive.** Arrange for alternate transportation to wherever you are going after the reception, well before your wedding day. If the reception is at a hotel, arrange to stay there overnight (many hotels will offer a free room if you hold your wedding reception on the premises).

2. **Have someone keep track of gifts, especially envelopes.** They can easily get misplaced or forgotten in all the excitement. Give this duty to someone you trust, like your best man or a parent.

1. **Kiss the bride.**

Index